DUAL DIAGNOSIS
COUNSELING THE MENTALLY ILL
SUBSTANCE ABUSER

Katie Evans, C.A.D.C., an Oregon board-certified Alcohol and Drug Counselor, completed her undergraduate work in sociology at the University of Oregon. Ms. Evans is consultant on dual diagnosis and program development for the West Coast region of Samissa Health Care Corporation, and has been both counselor and clinical director for inpatient and outpatient dual diagnosis treatment programs for both adults and adolescents. She has practiced a program of continuous recovery from addiction since 1983.

As President of Evans and Sullivan, Inc., an outpatient counseling program in Portland, Oregon, Ms. Evans works as a therapist and presents workshops and seminars nationally on the topics of dual diagnosis, antisocial personality disorders, and other treatment resistant populations. Her work with the dual diagnosis population has been published in national magazines. She is also co-author with J. Michael Sullivan of *Step Study Counseling with the Dual Disordered Client* (Hazelden Foundation).

J. Michael Sullivan, Ph.D., associate professor at the School of Professional Psychology at Pacific University, completed his undergraduate studies at Boston College and received his master's degree in psychology and his Ph.D. in clinical psychology from the University of Oregon. He is a licensed clinical psychologist and clinical director for the adult program at Pacific Gateway Hospital in Portland, Oregon, and has been the clinical director of both inpatient and outpatient mental health treatment programs serving adults as well as adolescents.

As Clinical Director of Evans and Sullivan, Inc., an outpatient counseling program in Portland, Oregon, Dr. Sullivan provides outpatient psychological services and presents workshops and seminars nationally on the topics of dual diagnosis, borderline personality, and other treatment resistant populations. Dr. Sullivan has published in the areas of dual diagnosis and personality disorders, and is also co-author with Katie Evans of *Step Study Counseling with the Dual Disordered Client* (Hazelden Foundation).

DUAL DIAGNOSIS
COUNSELING THE MENTALLY ILL SUBSTANCE ABUSER

Katie Evans, C.A.D.C.
J. Michael Sullivan, Ph.D.

THE GUILFORD PRESS
New York   London

© 1990 The Guilford Press
A Division of Guilford Publications, Inc.
72 Spring Street, New York, NY 10012

Printed in the United States of America.

This book is printed on acid-free paper.

Last digit in print number: 9 8 7 6 5 4 3 2 1

Library of Congress Cataloging-in-Publication Data

Evans, Katie.
   Dual diagnosis : a guide for counselors and case managers / Katie
Evans and J. Michael Sullivan.
     p. cm.
   Includes bibliographic references.
   ISBN 0-89862-436-3.—ISBN 0-89862-450-9(pbk)
   1. Alcoholics—Mental health. 2. Mentally ill—Alcohol use.
3. Alcoholics—Counseling of. 4. Mentally ill—Counseling of.
I. Sullivan, J. Michael. II. Title.
   [DNLM: 1. Counseling—methods. 2. Mental Disorders—
complications. 3. Substance Abuse—complications. 4. Substance
Dependence—complications.   WM 55 E923d]
RC565.E87 1990
616.86—dc20
DNLM/DLC
for Library of Congress   90-3036
                                       CIP

*This book is dedicated to the many individuals
who have acted as "Eskimos" (see p. 124) in our lives.
These men and women guided us, inspired us, and shared
with us their experience, strength, and hope.
Without the help of our "Eskimos," this book would
not have been possible. Thank you.*

Contents

Foreword

This book provides a much needed reference to chemical dependency counselors, social workers, family therapists, psychologists, psychiatrists, program directors, and other professionals concerned with the individual who is suffering from both a substance abuse disorder and a second, concurrent mental disorder. Katie Evans and Michael Sullivan address five key areas involving dual diagnosis: (1) the definition(s)—what is meant by "dual diagnosis"; (2) diagnosis—when and how to assess dual disorders; (3) treatment—the reasoning behind using an integrative model, and specific guidelines for treatment adolescent as well as adults; (4) aftercare—suggestions for family counseling, crisis situations, and relapse prevention; and (5) burnout—how to recognize and work through a common "trap" that can render even the best practitioner ineffective, frustrated, and/or too tired to continue what, otherwise, is excellent work.

In addition, they have presented the work in such a "user-friendly" format that the reader may find one or more sections immediately applicable in his/her own clinical practice or program.

I am also impressed with the authors' candor regarding their own experiences, biases, and limitations. For example, a detailed discussion of psychopharmacological issues related to the treatment of individuals with a dual diagnosis is limited to a few basic principles. At the same time, however, they encourage professional consultation with psychiatrists, and provide guidelines for making the best use of physicians experienced in mental health and addiction medicine.

Dual diagnosis is a relatively new, yet fast developing area of research. As a physician who specializes in this syndrome, I am pleased to see a text that offers a functional model for the present while we vigorously search for more answers.

RICHARD K. RIES, M.D.

ix

Preface

We have written this book in order to provide counselors and case managers with a general introduction to the assessment, treatment, and management of someone with a dual diagnosis. A "dual diagnosis" person is an individual with both a substance abuse or dependency problem and a coexisting psychiatric disorder. The focus of this book is to provide the reader with a greater understanding of the issues that dual diagnosis individuals present for counselors, case managers, and others, and to offer practical concepts and techniques that we have found useful in working with this population.

Service providers more and more often face the tasks of assessing, treating, and managing persons with dual diagnoses. Professionals have a growing awareness of the need to help these individuals with both sets of difficulties, and the numbers of persons with both a psychiatric disorder and a coexisting substance use or dependency problem are increasing. At the same time, individuals with dual diagnoses pose special challenges to service providers.

Several factors contribute to this challenge. The dual diagnosis individual has more than double trouble. Both problems interact in a fashion that compounds the person's distress and disability. Making accurate diagnoses and appropriate treatment decisions can be tricky. Denial is a cardinal feature of chemical abuse and dependency and of many psychiatric disorders. Dually diagnosed persons often exhibit dual denial and can be very resistant to treatment. Their dual problems also make them less amenable to conventional treatment approaches. Finally, dual diagnosis clients are at high risk for relapse with either their psychiatric disorder or their substance use problem or both.

Counseling and case managing dually diagnosed clients present other issues. Debate still exists about the best approach for counseling the chemically abusing or dependent individual and, in some cases, persons with certain psychiatric disorders. Dual diagnosis individuals can intensify this debate. Few agencies have the trained personnel and the range of services needed to treat someone with dual disorders. The available literature and research, although beginning to grow, are still limited. Studies of prevalence, incidence, and diagnostic issues are available, as are some descriptions of model programs, especially for the chronically mentally ill population. However, there are little data on psychiatric disorders that are not chronic conditions, on adolescents, and on the effectiveness of various treatment approaches designed for dual diagnosis individuals.

All this can cause counselors and case managers who are dedicated to helping their clients to feel frustrated and overwhelmed and to question their competence. We remember a phone call from one desperate mental health worker. Her supervisor had just told her that many of their chronically mentally ill clients had a drug problem and that she had to start a dual diagnosis program. She knew enough to know that she knew very little about chemical dependency. When she contacted the staff of the local community alcohol and drug program for assistance they had told her that they knew nothing about mental illness. "Help," she asked us, "What do I do?"

We have encountered the "What do I do?" question again and again in our treatment, consultation, and training contacts with a variety of providers serving dual diagnosis populations. Providers are always asking if we know of anything written that provides a general introduction to working with the dually diagnosed individual and practical approaches that are helpful to counselors and case managers as well as to family members and others working with dual diagnosis individuals. We hope that this book does just that.

We have accomplished our mission if this book helps our readers increase their ability to:

1. Discuss the unique clinical needs and treatment issues that the dual diagnosis client presents and articulate a helpful framework for working with this population.
2. Evaluate both the substance use problem and the psychiatric disorder of the dually diagnosed client.
3. Refer to appropriate treatment resources and to manage dual diagnosis cases.
4. Effectively counsel dually diagnosed adult and adolescent clients and their families.

5. Work comfortably and confidently with this difficult population.

We have intended this book primarily for direct-line human service providers. This includes not only mental health and chemical dependency professionals but also other providers who encounter dual diagnosis clients, such as court and child protective workers. However, other professionals such as physicians, psychologists, nurses, social workers, and even the families and friends of dually diagnosed individuals may also find much of the material here useful in understanding dually diagnosed persons and the issues involved in assessing and treating them.

Although we have kept in mind and utilized the available research, we have also relied on our clinical experience with close to a thousand dual diagnosis clients during the past 5 years in writing this book. We have emphasized concepts and techniques that we have found useful in working with dually diagnosed persons. When confronted with a question where there are conflicting or no research data, we have presented tentative answers that we feel work best for us and our clients. We place particular emphasis on the integration of cognitive-behavioral and the disease process and Twelve Step Recovery models as the most effective way we have found to work with these clients. Consistent with our recovery philosophy, we have chosen not to call chemical dependency a psychiatric disorder. We have also presented overviews of both chemical dependency and mental health concepts and practices and have included a glossary of our terms in the Appendix. In our experience few care providers are experts in both areas, and mental health and chemical dependency providers benefit from this "cross-training." To make the material interesting and accessible we have tried to use a down-to-earth writing style that combines humor and information and that minimizes extensive references in the body of the text. Instead, we have numbered references in the text and referenced them at the end of each chapter.

Some caveats are in order. We have changed details of case examples to protect confidentiality. We are also not physicians, and we base statements regarding medication on what we have learned from working with psychiatrists, nurse practitioners, and our clients. Always consult with qualified medical personnel regarding any medical issues. It is important to stress that it is helpful to obtain supervised experience in working with dual diagnosis clients. This book can be a good start, but counselors and case managers should consider pursuing additional training and supervision before treating persons with dual disorders alone. This text is not a comprehensive presentation of the entire field of chemical dependency and mental health. It is also not an exhaustive review of the research literature. These were not our goals. Instead, we have attempted to provide a general introduction to the field and its issues. We have provided references and suggested sources throughout the text for readers who wish to read more about these topics. We are currently working on additional books that give more detailed coverage of such issues as Twelve Step work with dually diagnosed individuals.

We wish to acknowledge J. Douglas Myers, Ph.D., for what he has taught us about working with dually diagnosed adolescents. We gratefully acknowledge Samissa Health Care Corporation and Pacific Gateway Hospital for their professional as well as personal support. And we acknowledge Community Psychiatric Centers and Dammasch State Hospital for providing us with the early foundation of our work.

KATIE EVANS
J. MICHAEL SULLIVAN

1

The Nature of the Problem

What do we mean when we say that this person has a "dual diagnosis"? For many years service professionals used this term to refer to persons who were mentally retarded or developmentally disabled and who also had a coexisting psychiatric disorder. However, professionals have more recently begun to use the term dual diagnosis to refer to a person with both a chemical abuse or dependency problem and a coexisting psychiatric disorder.

The *Diagnostic and Statistical Manual of Mental Disorders—Third Edition—Revised* (DSM-III-R) of the American Psychiatric Association is the prevailing standard for establishing psychiatric diagnoses acceptable in the professional community and for giving such a diagnosis to a given individual. The DSM-III-R generally defines a mental disorder as a clinically significant behavioral or psychological syndrome or pattern that occurs in an individual and that is typically associated with a painful symptom (distress) or impairment in one or more important areas of functioning (disability). There is also an inference that there is a behavioral, psychological, or biological dysfunction, that the disturbance is not only in the relationship between the individual and society, and that the difficulties are not transient (1).

The DSM-III-R also defines psychoactive substance abuse as a maladaptive pattern of use not meeting the criteria for dependence that has persisted for at least 1 month or has occurred repeatedly over a longer time period. An individual's use is maladaptive when the use causes or exacerbates a physical, psychological, social, or occupational problem or when there is repeated use in situations that may be

1

physically hazardous. The DSM-III-R notes that the abuse diagnosis is more likely to apply to individuals who have only recently started using psychoactive substances or who use substances less likely to be associated with withdrawal symptoms. The cardinal features of psychoactive substance dependence are continued use despite negative consequences and loss of control. The DSM-III-R criteria for this diagnosis require that symptoms last at least 1 month or show repeated occurrences over a longer period and that the person demonstrate at least three of the following: (1) use of greater amounts or for longer periods than the person intended; (2) persistent desire or unsuccessful efforts to cut down or stop; (3) large amount of time spent obtaining, using, or recovering from the use; (4) frequent intoxication or withdrawal symptoms when one is otherwise expected to fulfill role obligations or when use is physically hazardous; (5) important role or leisure activities reduced or abandoned because of substance use; (6) continued use despite its causing or exacerbating other problems; (7) tolerance, or the need to take increasing amounts of the substance to achieve the same effect; (8) withdrawal symptoms; (9) use to avoid withdrawal. Psychoactive substances include alcohol, barbituates or other sedative–hypnotics or anxiolytics, opiods such as heroin, stimulants such as amphetamines, cocaine, and crack. Also included are marijuana, tobacco, caffeine, inhalants, phencyclidine (PCP), and hallucinogens such as LSD. The dual diagnosis client meets the criteria for both chemical abuse or dependency and a coexisting psychiatric disorder.

DOUBLE TROUBLE

Why have professionals become increasingly interested in this population? Why have professionals appropriated the term dual diagnosis to describe psychiatric clients with a chemical abuse or dependency problem? Media reports indicate a veritable substance abuse epidemic in America during the last several decades. More people are using more and different kinds of chemicals and are using them at younger and younger ages. The chemicals abused include not only illegal substances but also the products of increasingly sophisticated biochemical research and development such as the minor tranquilizers. As the general population has had increasing access to, and use of psychoactive substances, so too have the individuals with a coexisting psychiatric disorder.

In fact, the available data suggest that individuals with a psychiatric disorder are at increased risk for having a substance abuse disorder.

Epidemiological studies (2) have suggested prevalence rates for alcohol and substance abuse or dependency of around 7% in the general population. However, individuals with a history of major depression or anxiety disorder appear to have double the risk for later substance abuse or dependence (3). Among young, chronically mentally ill patients, reported chemical abuse rates approach or exceed 50% (4,5). Other data suggest a 20% alcohol abuse rate for persons with a bipolar disorder and 70% rate for persons with an antisocial personality disorder (6). These numbers are likely to be conservative. Clinicians often fail to diagnose substance abuse in psychiatric patients (see Ref. 7), and studies using urine drug screens, at least among psychiatric inpatients, show that patients underreport their substance use (8,9).

The individual with a dual diagnosis presents with especially severe distress and disability. The dual diagnosis person's situation is one where the whole problem is greater than the sum of the parts, since the two disorders inevitably exacerbate each other. The confused person becomes more confused, the hostile person more threatening and assaultive, and the suicidal person more likely to engage in harmful activities. Individuals already having trouble functioning as family members and workers or students because of their psychiatric disorder show even more impairment when they abuse psychoactive chemicals. Clients with both disorders, for example, more frequently use hospital emergency rooms and require hospitalization (see Refs. 10,11). Alcoholics who also have a major depression have more suicide attempts, and alcoholics with antisocial personalities have more legal and social problems (12). Drug abusers with chronic psychotic symptoms have more psychiatric difficulties and worse occupational outcome over a 10-year period (13).

Coexisting disorders are also more difficult to treat. Achieving a valid diagnostic assessment and deciding on appropriate treatments is difficult (14,15). Individuals abusing or dependent on drugs can develop symptoms similar to those seen in many psychiatric disorders. These include psychotic symptoms, depression, anxiety, mood swings, isolation and social withdrawal, as well as erratic, hostile, or self-centered relationships and criminal behavior. On the other hand, the person with uncontrolled mania or the individual with an anxiety disorder will often escalate his or her use of psychoactive substances as symptoms become more acute (12). Several questions then face the evaluator. Are this person's problems caused mainly by the chemicals or the psychiatric disorder or both? Will the client better be served in a mental health or a chemical dependency program? Or does he/she need a special dual diagnosis program, and, if so, where do I find one?

Getting the dual diagnosis person to agree to or comply with treatment can also be difficult. Alcoholics and addicts often do not admit that they have an abuse problem when asked and, instead, minimize their use and associated problems and/or generate excuses for their behavior. Many individuals with psychiatric disorders also rationalize their difficulties away or blame others. The person with schizophrenia who has psychotic symptoms and is convinced of an FBI "plot," the manic person who is a little too "A-OK!" and the antisocial person who states that "everyone does it and only he got caught" are often not willing or able to identify themselves as needing help. Add the two disorders together, and dual diagnosis persons often show double denial and even less willingness or ability to participate in treatment than the individual with a single diagnosis.

Dually diagnosed persons can also lack social connections such as an involved family or a good job that might provide the motivation to seek and cooperate with any treatment plan. Many dually diagnosed persons are, in addition, unable to comply with treatment or to benefit from standard interventions because of the complication of both illnesses. Understanding lectures on the negative effects of drugs is difficult for those people with impaired concentration. Attending self-help groups is hard for persons who are seriously depressed and find it difficult to get out of bed or for persons who are paranoid and are convinced others are talking about them. The person who suffers from schizophrenia and who drinks will tend to forget to take the prescribed antipsychotic medication, and the sedated person with a personality disorder will often miss clinic appointments. Intense and demanding confrontations of the sort often used with persons who are "just" alcoholic or addicted will sometimes increase the psychotic symptoms or suicidal ideation of dual diagnosis persons (16–18).

Working with dual diagnosis persons can be straining and draining. The intensity of their problems can lead providers to feel scared, discouraged, or alienated. Providers trained in working with one type of population sometimes feel unprepared to treat the wide range of problems that these clients present. Relapse is a common occurrence (see Chapter 9), leading providers (and families) to feel that their efforts are a waste of time and that matters are hopeless.

SYSTEMS IN CONFLICT

Philosophical conflicts and a fragmented service system can further compound the difficulites facing providers, dually diagnosed persons, and their families. Society has tended to view alcoholism and addiction as moral and legal issues. Individuals with chemical use difficulties are seen as "bad" people who lack will power and suffer from a defective character. The recent "Just Say No" campaign and the emphasis on fines, jail, and sending in the Marines reflect this point of view. Similarly, society has historically tended to view many mental disorders as the result of poor motivation or a weak constitution. The individual who suffers from either chemical dependency or psychiatric disorder faces the stigma and shame associated with his/her illness and often receives advice that says "Snap out of it!" This is doubly true for dually diagnosed clients.

Mental health professionals have historically taken a different tack, preferring to see mental disorders as illness and reframing the psychiatric patient as sick and not "bad." But many mental health professionals also viewed alcoholism and addiction not as illnesses in their own right but as symptoms of an underlying psychiatric disorder. Whether a matter of an addictive personality, of an underlying depression, or one of self-medication, the chemical abuse or dependency problem would disappear with treatment of the "real" problem through the use of psychotherapy, medication, or other mental health treatment, according to this point of view. Even when mental health professionals did focus on the alcoholism or addiction, they found the alcoholic or addict difficult to engage and maintain in treatment and to be highly prone to relapse. Some mental health professionals even decided that chemically abusing or dependent persons were untreatable and excluded them from services.

Alcoholics Anonymous, in contrast, defined alcoholism (and by extension other substance-use problems) as a primary, physiologically based, progressive, and chronic disease. This disease had not only negative physical and psychosocial consequences but also negative spiritual effects. The solution was commitment to abstinence, social support through A.A., and working a recovery program based on the Twelve Steps. Some A.A. members also viewed the mental health establishment with suspicion. Too many of them had received medication, electroshock therapy, or years of psychotherapy to no avail. Sometimes mental health professionals did not ask patients about their drinking, and the alcoholic/addict did not share with the professional accurate information regarding drinking or drug use patterns.

More recently, professionals concerned primarily with alcoholism and addiction have gained increased recognition and independence. Although other approaches to addiction such as aversive conditioning have been developed, the A.A. recovery model has become more influential. An increasing amount of research focuses on the physiological basis of addiction (see Ref. 19), and a growing number of publications extend and refine recovery concepts. Chemical dependency professionals have established training and treatment programs founded on these concepts. Governments have established offices of substance abuse independent of their mental health offices. Funding sources, including government agencies and insurance carriers, have established separate funding for chemical dependency treatment. But despite these recent advances, philosophical and theoretical conflicts are not uncommon. Service delivery systems tend also to focus on treating either the mental health problem or the chemical dependency but not both.

Dual diagnosis clients and providers have inherited this legacy. Some mental health professionals refuse to treat alcoholics and addicts, even those with a coexisting psychiatric disorder, seeing them as resistant to traditional mental health approaches or as unlikely to benefit from treatment as long as they continue to use substances. If they do treat them, these professionals sometimes tend to focus only on the coexisting psychiatric disorder.

Some chemical dependency counselors, on the other hand, downplay the need to treat the psychiatric disorder. This is especially true regarding client use of psychotropic medication, which many chemical dependency counselors view as mood-altering and hence fatal to a person's recovery. Some of these professionals will often refuse to treat the dual diagnosis client on medication.

Other divisions persist. Typically there are separate programs and staff for the treatment of psychiatric and chemical dependency disorders, and few professionals have the necessary cross-training. Governments continue to have separate departments for mental health and for alcohol and drug matters and have difficulty making the necessary legislative changes. Separate training programs are the norm. Funding sources provide different benefit levels for the two sets of disorders, and funding for nontraditional programs is in short supply. Meanwhile the courts mix the moral and need-for-treatment approaches. We now look at some of these issues in more detail.

MENTAL HEALTH CENTERS

With the rampant spread of drug abuse in our society at large, it is not surprising to learn that individuals who are already experiencing nervous and mental problems that keep them from being productive, happy members of our society are heavy users of drugs and alcohol.

Many of these individuals receive disability money from the federal or state government because of their inability to function in the workplace. Without employment, members of this group find themselves with many idle hours. They often feel worthless and unproductive, and they know they do not "fit in" as do their nondisabled fellows.

It is not difficult to feel as though you belong in the world of drugs and alcohol. A bar stool and a bottle of beer are the only requirement for membership at the local tavern. The drug dealers value their money the same as others', and although dually diagnosed individuals are frequently taken advantage of by the unscrupulous drug dealer, they still have no difficulty obtaining illegal drugs.

The use of chemicals by persons with a mental disorder exacerbates their illness and makes them very poor candidates for case management of the mental illness without special treatment. In many states the community mental health system is not set up to address any alcohol or drug abuse. If a provider identifies a substance abuse problem, the provider typically refers the client to another agency that specializes in alcohol and drug treatment. Financial assistance and counseling services for the mental illness may be terminated at this time. Finding a program or agency that is able or willing to treat this client presents a whole other set of challenges.

PUBLIC DRUG AND ALCOHOL PROGRAMS

With national attention focused on substance abuse, federal and state agencies have earmarked money to be used to provide assessment and treatment services to indigent adults and youth. Each state, county, and community agency utilizes these funds to meet the identified need in its area. When mentally ill clients present themselves at the community alcohol program for assessment and treatment, several problems arise.

An intoxicated individual claiming to hear voices is often thought to be in need of detox in the absence of a documented history of mental illness to suggest otherwise. These individuals often deny not only that they have problems with drinking or using drugs, but they also deny that they have any history of psychiatric problems. The chemical dependency counselor's logical course of action is to admit such a client to a community detox center in order to begin rehabilitation care for the substance abuse problem. Shortly into detox, it becomes clear that the client's problems are more complicated. The client demonstrates strange and psychotic behavior. When the overworked social worker attempts to transfer the client to the state hospital, he/she learns that "hearing voices" doesn't meet the criteria for commitment to the hospital and that an individual must be "dangerous to self and others.'' With no other recourse, the provider discharges the client, still psychotic and addicted, from the detox center and refers the client to a local community mental health agency. And the cycle begins once again.

THE LEGAL SYSTEM

For the dually diagnosed client the relationship between substance abuse and criminal activity is itself a matter of concern. The use of illegal drugs in and of itself is criminal in most states. It is highly unlikely that the average dually diagnosed client surviving on a welfare disability payment can support any kind of regular drug use without resorting to crime. Burglary and theft are the most common ways for the drug abuser to obtain money. For the psychiatrically impaired individual, the ability to mastermind a serious crime or consistently engage in criminal activity without getting caught is extremely unlikely.

Once apprehended, the police often arrest the individual and the client enters the criminal justice system. The court system is not designed to serve as a treatment alternative for the mentally ill client. Following arraignment, the client is usually released pending a hearing and returns to the community untreated.

SYSTEMS IN CONFLICT—A CASE EXAMPLE

The following case illustrates some of the issues we've discussed. Tim, an 18-year-old male suffering from schizophrenia, was receiving voluntary treatment through an outpatient community mental health center. Tim was receiving Prolixin® shots, as he found the oral medication a ''hassle.'' His case manager had become concerned that Tim might be experimenting with marijuana. Tim was starting to miss appointments and his parents reported that he was hanging out with some negative adolescents in the neighborhood. When Tim did appear for an appointment he was moody, avoidant, and displayed an increasingly negative attitude toward the case manager. The case manager scheduled a meeting for Tim and his parents. Tim did not show up for the appointment. Tim's parents met with the counselor and discussed an incident in which they had found Tim smoking marijuana in his room. Tim's parents felt it was ''a stage'' and were not alarmed by the incident. The case manager referred Tim to an outpatient chemical dependency program for an evaluation. Tim did not show up for the appointment. When the case manager tried to contact Tim's parents to reschedule, they informed the case manager that they would be taking Tim to "another clinic" for his medication and wanted the case manager to close Tim's file.

Two weeks following the closure of his case, Tim was arrested. High on drugs and off his medication, Tim had stolen a city bus and smashed into two parked cars and a police vehicle. Tim was lodged in the County Jail, where he had to be placed into five-point restraints because of his psychosis and violent behavior.

YOUTH AT RISK

Previous discussion in this chapter cited concerns and systems conflicts regarding adults with a major mental disorder. Although Chapter 7 will take an in-depth look at assessment and treatment of adolescents, this population deserves comment. In the case of adolescents, the issue of dual disorders presents itself in a slightly different light. Child protective services experts report that in the vast majority of all child abuse cases the perpetrator was abusing drugs or alcohol. An environment where abuse of chemicals and violence is present is a breeding ground for emotional and psychological problems in children.

Social workers working in the area of child protective services who identify parental substance abuse as a problem have no authority to require parents to seek help. The judicial authority granted child protective service workers is through the juvenile court system, which has statute authority only over the child. A social worker and/or court worker can request only that a child not be allowed to return home. He/she cannot demand parental compliance with treatment. Children marked by the pain of their own sexual or physical abuse often turn to drugs and alcohol to relieve the pain of living. The depression, guilt, and anger that engulf the child are multiplied by the use of chemicals. With a family history of alcoholism likely, it does not take an adolescent long to enter the process of his own addiction.

FINANCIAL COST

With government budget deficits a concern and social programs a low priority, public funds for treatment are limited. Who will pay for the necessary care? In some cases it is private health insurance carriers who authorize payment for the chemical dependency, mental health care, or both. But even those originally with resources find themselves depleted with the multiple treatment failures experienced by the dually diagnosed client. Sadly, in other cases no treatment is available so clients find themselves being shuffled from one system to another.

COST TO FAMILIES

Family members and relatives of the dually diagnosed person will often find themselves depleted emotionally and financially. Their attempts to find adequate care for their loved one is often met with a breakdown of "the system" to assist in public sector treatment programs. Private sector programs, although sometimes available, place a tremendous financial burden on the family, and cannot guarantee a positive outcome from treatment. The substance-abusing, psychiatrically disordered family member moves from crisis to crisis, stretching thin the patience and tolerance of even the most supportive family. The dual diagnosis individual can become violent and threatening toward family. This can force the family to shut out the person in order to protect themselves and other family members. Other families continue to support their family member from one unsuccessful treatment to the next, sharing the heartbreak of this perceived failure.

CLIENT PAIN

Stricken by the disease of chemical dependency and suffering from a psychiatric disorder, the dually diagnosed individual is not well armed to deal with system's conflicts. Persons enter expensive private psychiatric hospitals, where treatment professionals may not address their substance abuse problems. The same persons enter private chemical dependency programs where their mental health issues may be put on hold until sobriety is established. The dually diagnosed person has a difficult time obtaining sobriety for any length of time without getting help for the coexisting psychiatric problems. Each unsuccessful treatment experience adds to the person's confusion and exaggerated feelings of worthlessness. With neither illness adequately treated, the client moves closer to the ultimate end of institutionalization or untimely death.

CONCLUSION

Dually diagnosed persons represent a seriously distressed and disabled population that is growing in numbers and whose coexisting illnesses are difficult to treat. Conflicting treatment philosophies and fragmented service systems sometimes compound these problems. Providers have started to use the term "dual diagnosis" to designate a clinical population experiencing two sets of problems. The use of the term dual diagnosis also attempts to signal others that these clients have special needs and require specialized treatment approaches. The following chapters attempt to provide some solutions to some of the problems raised in this chapter, with an emphasis on the clinical aspects of the dually diagnosed individual's situation.

REFERENCES

1. American Psychiatric Association. *Diagnostic and Statistical Manual of Mental Disorders, third edition, revised.* American Psychiatric Association, Washington, D.C., 1987.
2. Myers, J. K., Weissman, M. M., Tischler, G. L., et al. Six month prevalence of psychiatric disorders in three communities. *Archives of General Psychiatry, 41,* 959–967, 1984.
3. Christie, K. A., Burke, J. D., Regier, D. A., et al. Epidemiologic evidence for early onset of mental disorders and higher risk of drug abuse in young adults. *American Journal of Psychiatry, 148(8),* 971–975, 1988.
4. Bergman, H. C., and Harris, M. Substance abuse among young chronic patients. *Psychosocial Rehabilitation Journal, 9(1),* 49–54, 1985.
5. Safer, D. Substance abuse by young adult chronic patients. *Hospital and Community Psychiatry, 38(5),* 511–514, 1987.
6. Schukit, M. A. Genetic and clinical implications of alcoholism and affective disorder. *American Journal of Psychiatry, 143(2),* 140–147, 1986.
7. Ananth, J., Vandewater, S., Kamal, M., et al. Missed diagnosis of substance abuse in psychiatric patients. *Hospital and Community Psychiatry, 40(3),* 297–299, 1989.
8. Ranzani, J., Farina, F., and Stern K. Covert drug abuse among patients hospitalized in the psychiatric ward of a university hospital. *International Journal of the Addictions, 10(4),* 693–698, 1975.
9. Crowley, T. J., Chesluk, D., Dilts, S., and Hart, R. Drug and alcohol abuse among psychiatric admissions. *Archives of General Psychiatry, 30,* 13–20, 1974.
10. Pensker, H. Addicted patients in hospital psychiatric units. *Psychiatric Annals, 13,* 619–623, 1983.
11. Trier, T. R., and Levy, R. J. Emergency, urgent and elective admissions: Studies in a general hospital psychiatric emergency service. *Archives of General Psychiatry, 21,* 423–430, 1969.
12. Schuckit, M. A. The clinical implications of primary diagnostic groups among alcoholics. *Archives of General Psychiatry, 42,* 1043–1049, 1985.
13. Perkins, K. A., Simpson, J. C., and Tsuang, M. T. Ten year followup of

drug abusers with acute or chronic psychosis. *Hospital and Community Psychiatry, 37(5)*, 481–484, 1986.

14. Hall, R., Popken, M. K., DeVane, R., and Stickney, S. K. The effects of unrecognized drug abuse in psychiatric patients. *Journal of Diseases of the Nervous System, 36*, 550–553, 1975.

15. Kranzler, H. R., and Liebowitz, N. R. Anxiety and depression in substance abuse. *Medical Clinics of North America, 72(4)*, 867–885, 1988.

16. Salzman, B. Substance abuse with psychiatric problems. In J. H. Lowinson and P. Ruiz (Eds.), *Substance Abuse: Clinical Problems and Perspectives.* Williams & Wilkins, Baltimore, 1981.

17. Stren, M. L., and Solberg, K. B. Maximum hospital benefits vs. against medical advice: A comparative study. *Archives General Psychiatry, 22*, 351–355, 1970.

18. McLellan, A. T., Luborsky, L., Woody, G. E., et al. Predicting response to alcohol and drug abuse treatment: Role of psychiatric severity. *Archives of General Psychiatry, 40*, 620–625, 1983.

19. Searles, J. S. The role of genetics in the pathogenesis of alcoholism. *Journal of Abnormal Psychology, 97(2)*, 152–167, 1988.

2

Models of Treatment and
Their Integration

In this chapter we outline common treatment approaches for chemical
dependency and for mental health disorders. We then detail our own
integrated model for working with dual diagnosis clients and argue for
its utility. We also examine other model approaches and present the
little outcome data available. Finally, we discuss the problems associated with integrating mental health and chemical dependency points
of view in treatment organizations and suggest possible solutions for
dealing with these barriers.

MODELS OF CHEMICAL ABUSE AND DEPENDENCY TREATMENT

Different approaches to the treatment of chemical abuse and dependency exist, and there is no universal consensus on the best model for
treating all clients. One controversial difference involves the goal of
treatment. Should the counselor emphasize total abstinence from all
mood-altering chemicals, or should controlled use be the goal of
treatment? In the literature these discussions typically focus on alcohol
use. Few professionals would advocate the "controlled" use of heroin
or crack, although we have very occasionally encountered a counselor
or case manager who feels that controlled use of marijuana is relatively
benign. Professionals arguing for controlled use typically make a
distinction between problem drinkers and true alcoholics, cite studies

14   CHAPTER 2

showing controlled use by formerly alcoholic or addicted persons, and/or feel that it is better to attempt this goal with clients unwilling to accept abstinence rather than have troubled clients receive no help at all (see Ref. 1).

Several different approaches to treating abuse and addiction also exist. The traditional view holds that the person's problematic chemical involvement is really a symptom of, or a response to, a psychiatric disorder or family dysfunction (2,3). There are several variations of this theme. The so-called "alcoholic" personality type was a popular one for many years. Clinicians dealing with persons who had alcohol or drug problems experienced them as angry, self-centered, immature, blaming, and excuse-making. Clinicians then assumed that individuals with these personality styles (seen as stemming from early childhood experiences) were especially vulnerable to the emotional effects of alcohol and lacked the ego strength to forego alcohol's pleasure. Another popular variation is the notion of self-medication. This view holds that the alcoholic or addicted person abuses chemicals in a well-meaning but problem-producing attempt to alleviate the psychic pain and manage the symptoms of the underlying problem. A more recent approach assumes that the alcoholic or addicted individual is really responding to marital conflict or other family dysfunctions. The implication of this symptom-of-something-else notion is straightforward, at least in theory. Successfully treat the underlying problem, and the client will moderate or stop his/her chemical abuse.

Other approaches focus on the chemical use and dependency as an independent problem in its own right. Behavioral interventions constitute one such set of approaches. These include aversive conditioning, where the sight, smell, and taste of alcohol is paired with a noxious stimulus such as an electric shock or chemically induced vomiting (5). Other behavior therapies include skills training approaches, where clients learn improved ways to monitor and manage their drinking behavior through use of written journals of drinking patterns, substituting slowed drinking rates, and arranging for rewards for modified use (see Ref. 6). Another set of approaches relies on medications such as Antabuse® (disulfiram) to produce an aversive reaction to any alcohol used or methadone maintanence to block withdrawal symptoms and any euphoric effects from opiate use, all without any high being induced by the medication itself.

Educational approaches, either alone or in combination with other approaches, are very commonly used. Counselors and case managers typically advise clients to moderate or stop their abuse, give informational lectures and reading materials about the negative impact of chemical use, and perhaps even give objective and detailed feedback regarding the status and severity of problems related to the chemical use such as physical complications or neurological impairment (see Ref. 7). The intent of the educational approach is to motivate clients to change their use behavior. Treatment programs also typically employ psychosocial therapy and rehabilitation interventions to address interpersonal and role dysfunctions commonly found among individuals with a chemical use or dependency problem (8).

The next section describes another approach in great detail because of its growing influence on the field and on our own approach to dual diagnosis clients.

THE RECOVERY MODEL

The increasingly predominant approach to treating chemical dependency uses the recovery model, a philosophy and treatment approach that views chemical dependency as a disease. It is chronic (it does not go away), it is progressive (it worsens with time), and it is fatal.

The American Medical Association has supported the belief that chemical dependency is a disease for three decades. In spite of more than 30 years of this support, many professionals do not believe or understand how chemical dependency can be a disease.

The behavior of an alcoholic or addict can be so distasteful and painful to those around him/her that the emotions evoked are not that of wanting to "care for a sick friend." In addition, so many people who have had the unfortunate experience of living with a practicing alcoholic or addict know how anger and even hatred are common experiences. With all of these negative emotions and difficult experiences with alcoholics and addicts, people tend to see these individuals as "bad" instead of "sick." It is for precisely this reason that an approach that treats chemically dependent people like "sick people getting well," not "bad people getting good," is useful.

The "disease process" recovery model provides a safe and supportive treatment framework free of moralizing and condemnation. The recovery model assists the chemically dependent person to look at his/her old "bad" behavior and reframe it as "sick" behavior. Slogans such as "one day at a time" and "easy does it" allow the alcoholic to see that he/she is now on a journey, a journey of recovery.

The recovery model states that an alcoholic is never "recovered." Instead they are "recovering." The disease is chronic. In order for one to stay on the journey of recovery there are certain events that need to occur. To begin the journey the alcoholic or addict needs to identify him/herself as an alcoholic or addict. Failure to accept that one suffers from the disease of chemical dependency will most certainly lead to a return to drinking and drug-abusing behaviors. Persons need to learn about the signs and symptoms of their disease as part of this process and to accept that they suffer from this disease.

In addition, information regarding damage done to body, mind, and spirit (as well as to family members) needs to be provided to assist the person in understanding that chemical dependency is dangerous and chronic. The disease lurks in wait for that person to take the first pill, fix, or drink. Abstinence is absolutely mandatory before any recovery can begin. The chemically dependent person must also understand that use of any mood-altering chemicals will most likely lead to addiction to a new drug or a return to old patterns of addiction.

The alcoholic or addict must also learn about cross-tolerance and addiction. One of the features of alcoholism is *metabolic tolerance*. This phenomenon is the body's adaptation response to the presence of alcohol. As this process occurs the body learns to tolerate larger doses of alcohol without experiencing the effects associated with increased use. The symptom of tolerance is one way to distinguish a social drinker from an alcoholic. The middle-stage alcoholic can frequently "drink everyone under the table" while showing only mild signs of intoxication. For the person who has a metabolic adaptation, the use of any central nervous system depressant will produce the same effects. The normally prescribed dosage of Valium®, Xanax®, Dalmane®, or other sedative-type drugs will have minimal effect on the alcoholic. We have been told by recovering alcoholics who had been in car wrecks or had surgery that they had difficulty becoming sedated or anesthetized because of this phenomenon. Because alcohol is a depressant drug like tranquilizers and sedatives it is imperative that recovering alcoholics steer clear of all mood-altering drugs in attempts to protect their sobriety. It is not uncommon to hear "recovering" alcoholics discuss how they were prescribed Xanax for a panic disorder, or used other chemicals when not drinking, only to find that they now had become addicted to this drug. This phenomenon is known as *cross-addiction*. In our experience alcoholics and addicts will also often switch their "drug of choice" to other classes of chemicals outside the depressant category and establish new addictions to other chemicals.

It is important to remember that chemical dependency is a *disease*. The physiological aspects lead the body to process and metabolize all chemicals differently than the nonaddicted person. Therefore, a safe and successful recovery program needs to be based on abstinence from *all* mood-altering chemicals. Acceptance of and belief that one suffers from a disease is paramount. No true recovery can begin without this belief. Remember, addiction is a *primary* urge. It takes precedence over relationships, money, food, and shelter. One doesn't wake up one morning and say to oneself, "Gee, today I think I'll stop doing the one thing that is most important to my life." Not unless there is a good reason! Acceptance that the disease of addiction is progressive and fatal can help a client realistically look at his/her drinking and using behavior. Alcoholics Anonymous states that "jails, institutions, and death" await the practicing addict.

In addition to education about the disease and its effects, peer support as well as peer confrontation are important. Using chemicals leads addicts to develop a skewed sense of themselves and their relationship to the world. Peers can point out unrealistic views of self and world and can assist the addict to gain needed emotional growth, growth stunted by the use of drugs and alcohol.

Skills building activities and other psychosocial therapies are very important. The disease of addiction prevents the individual from learning social and other coping skills and causes other problems. Assertiveness training and stress management can be an excellent start, as is family counseling. Abstinence is the start of recovery, but more is needed.

Discussion of the recovery model would be incomplete without a discussion of the Twelve Steps. The founders of Alcoholics Anonymous developed the Twelve Steps as a guide or "steps" to recovery. Dr. Bob and Bill W. were the cofounders of A.A. They joined together to help each other stay sober. Both had been unsuccessfully treated by various professionals and knew there was more involved with their own alcoholism than a lack of will power. They identified alcoholism as a disease and began the first meeting of Alcoholics Anonymous to try to help each other stay sober. The Twelve Steps they developed were a "program for recovery." They knew that acknowledgment and acceptance of their own illness was the beginning of the road to recovery. They also knew that a recovery program had to address other aspects of the disease.

Below are the steps of Alcoholics Anonymous and an explanation of the meaning of the steps. They are "suggestive only." Dr. Bob and Bill W. understood the willful nature of the alcoholic.

The Twelve Steps of A.A.*

1. "We admitted we were powerless over alcohol—that our lives had become unmanageable."

Those who have had experience with Step 1 understand the paradox of this step. By admitting powerlessness the individual becomes empow-

---

*The Twelve Steps reprinted with permission of Alcoholics Anonymous World Services, Inc.   A.A. is a program of recovery from alcoholism only. There are programs patterned after A.A. which address other problems.

ered to make healthy choices for him/herself. Most chemically dependent people have made countless vain attempts to control their alcohol and drug use and be a "social" drinker or user. Identifying that, in spite of all their efforts to control the uncontrollable, they eventually lost control provides the foundation on which chemically dependent persons can build their recovery. The alcoholic or addict must truly believe that his/her use of chemicals and the consequences of their use point to a disease process which they are powerless to control. The surrender of all this control releases the alcoholic/addict from a heavy burden. By labeling themselves as recovering addicts and alcoholics, these people begin to accept that they suffer from a disease that is chronic, progressive, fatal, and without a cure. Only a remission is possible, and this can only be achieved through abstinence.

2. "Came to believe that a power greater than ourselves could restore us to sanity."

Step 2 establishes hope and faith in an individual whose life has in recent times greatly lacked either commodity. The mention of a power greater than ourselves helps the addict/alcoholic to begin looking for help from others, which is a decidedly different strategy from the "leave me alone, I'll do it myself" attitude so common in the chemically dependent client. The "insanity" referred to in this step attempts to begin to address what is referred to as "stinking thinking." This is the denial and antisocial, self-centered world view of the practicing alcoholic, which once identified is slowly chipped away with continual and ongoing involvement with working the Twelve Steps and participation in Twelve Step programs.

3. "Made a decision to turn our will and our lives over to the care of God, *as we understood Him.*"

Step 3 helps the alcoholic to learn to "turn over" or let go of problems or worry over which the alcoholic has no control. Obsessive worry and fear tend to paralyze the alcoholic and make clear thinking and good problem solving extremely difficult. In order to turn something over, it is necessary to have a concept of who or what you are going to turn it over to. This step clearly states "God as we understood Him." This leaves open the opportunity for a variety of choices for who or what "God" is to the chemically dependent person as an individual. Many individuals raised in the Christian tradition chose the God of their childhood upbringing. Those who are perhaps rebelling from it establish their own personal concept of a higher power. Many alcoholics/addicts choose their A.A. or N.A. group as a collective higher power. Who or what the higher power is must always be the choice of the individual. Alcoholics Anonymous and Narcotics Anonymous are spiritual programs, not organized religion. They do not require a belief in a prescribed higher power.

4. "Made a searching and fearless moral inventory of ourselves."

The moral inventory described in this step is the process by which alcoholics can become relieved of their heavy burden of anger, resentment, fear, and guilt. A written inventory whereby the alcoholic or addict takes a look at how he or she was often the maker of his or her own problems is generally the best. This spiritual, emotional, and psychological housecleaning lightens the emotional load of the alcoholic or addict.

5. "Admitted to God, to ourselves, and to another human being the exact nature of our wrongs."

In this step the chemically dependent person discusses the content of the fourth step with another person as well as with the "higher power." By freely discussing the hidden burden, the power of old secrets is dissolved, and open, honest communication is made possible.

6. "Were entirely ready to have God remove all these defects of character."

This step readies the chemically dependent person for change. Realizing where he/she erred in the past makes the alcoholic ready to seek help from other places including a higher power. To change these destructive patterns is the goal of Step 6.

7. "Humbly asked Him to remove our shortcomings."

This step is the beginning of humility and true self-esteem. Bragging, grandiose ways of relating to the world are exchanged for humility and the beginnings of peace of mind.

8. "Made a list of all persons we had harmed, and became willing to make amends to them all."

Growing spiritually, the alcoholic becomes very aware of how the alcoholic and addictive behavior was hurtful not only to him/herself but to others. In this step the alcoholic makes a list of all those people he or she has harmed and is now willing to try to make amends and apologize for previous behaviors.

9. "Made direct amends to such people wherever possible, except when to do so would injure them or others."

In this step the alcoholic makes direct amends and apologizes to those individuals wronged previously by his or her destructive behavior.

Through this process the alcoholic/addict continues to build humility and gains peace of mind by cleaning up the wreckage of the past.

10. "Continued to take personal inventory, and when we were wrong promptly admitted it."

This is a maintenance step. By keeping a clean house through working an honest program, the alcoholic keeps from falling into old behaviors that can lead to relapse back into drinking and using behavior.

11. "Sought through prayer and meditation to improve our conscious contact with God *as we understood Him*, praying only for knowledge of His will for us and the power to carry that out."

The alcoholic now begins more fully to comprehend spirituality. He or she has conscious contact with a higher power and peace of mind that comes with knowing that things will work out the way they are supposed to.

12. "Having had a spiritual awakening as the result of these steps, we tried to carry this message to alcoholics, and to practice these principles in all our affairs."

The alcoholic is now transformed from the rigid, angry, controlling person he/she once was to an individual who understands serenity. With a feeling of purpose and usefulness in relationship to the world, the alcoholic becomes altruistic and will now try to help other suffering (or practicing) alcoholic/addicts to achieve sobriety and serenity with their own personal recovery program. Through the sharing of their own experiences, they help other alcoholics stop drinking and/or using drugs while at the same time strengthening their own commitment to sobriety.

There is much discussion in the chemical dependency field on whether or not someone is "working a program." There are five key elements to working a recovery program. They are:

1. Abstinence—no further ingestion of mind- or mood altering substances.
2. Going to meetings—regular attendance at Twelve Step recovery meetings such as Alcoholics Anonymous or Narcotics Anonymous. Ninety meetings in 90 days is a common suggestion for newly recovering persons.
3. Working the steps—this means really studying the steps and achieving a psychological, emotional, and spiritual under-

standing of the Twelve Steps. Written "stepwork" may be a tool to help familiarize someone with the Twelve Steps.
4. Sponsorship—this is where a member of A.A. or N.A. with usually one or more years of sobriety acts as a guide and mentor to the newly recovering person. Sponsors give ongoing one-on-one feedback to help guide a fellow A.A. member by sharing their experience, strength, and hope.
5. Meditation and prayer—the recovering person's newly developed spirituality is explored and strengthened.

EVALUATION OF TREATMENT APPROACHES

The approaches described in the last two section are those currently available to the counselor or case manager seeking to select an approach to the chemical-use problem of the dual diagnosis client. As mentioned earlier, no approach to the treatment of chemical dependency totally dominates the field. Although still influential, the traditional mental health view has recently decreased in its impact on the field, partly because of increasing research data that indicate that chemical use and withdrawal symptoms can cause psychiatric difficulties and family conflict (see Refs. 9,10) and partly because of the availability of other models. No approach has proven 100% effective with all clients (see Ref. 11), and differences in philosophy sometimes preclude a common definition of success. For example, the disease process model would argue that abstinence alone is not a total measure of recovery.

Differences among clients seem to account for some differences in outcome. Some individuals who "only" abuse chemicals appear to benefit from a purely educational approach in stopping or moderating their use (12,13). Individuals showing more clear-cut signs of dependency appear to benefit from more intensive approaches with a goal of abstinence (see Refs. 14,15).

Given these data, the treatment professionals will most likely select a particular approach for the substance use problem of their dual diagnosis clients based on available resources, client need and characteristics, and sympathy for the philosophy of a given approach. The counselor and case manager will also know that no approach is likely to guarantee total success with all clients.

THE MENTAL HEALTH MODEL

The mental health field encompasses an enormous variety of problems and approaches, and any summary overview runs the risk of glossing over important differences in point of view. Nonetheless, we can generate an overview of principles and practices commonly accepted by the majority of mental health professionals.

A majority of clinicians subscribe to the biopsychosocial model of psychiatric disorders. Although the exact weight of different factors-varies from disorder to disorder, this model specifies that psychiatric disorders have biological, psychological, and social components. These components include both the causes and consequences of each disorder. A corollary of this model is that interventions must address these components in a combined, comprehensive fashion that targets specific components in order to achieve success. For example, schizophrenia appears to be a brain disease with a genetic basis that results in a derangement of both the process and content of thinking as a primary feature. Associated features include oddities of feeling and behavior and impaired interpersonal and role functioning. Highly emotional, demanding interpersonal encounters as well as other stressors can exacerbate the condition. Interventions include medication to improve the process of thinking and the use of structure and skills training to address behavioral deficiencies. Other interventions include work with the family to help them cope with the sick family member. The creation of social support systems helps to maintain and enhance client gains.

As this example illustrates, complex disorders require comprehensive interventions. Mental health providers commonly draw on seven sets of strategies and tactics for their interventions. These include:

1. Correcting physiological deficiencies through such approaches as medication, nutritional supplements, and even exercise.
2. Building social support systems through such things as case management, attendance at special issue support groups, and mobilization of friendship networks.
3. Improving family functioning through such means as education about the disorder, communication skills training, and negotiation of contracts regarding roles, boundaries, and consequences for specified behaviors.
4. Prompting and reinforcing positive behavior through such tools as reminder cards, behavior checklists, and point systems.
5. Increasing the client's functional abilities through the teaching of such skills as assertion, stress management, or activities of daily living such as taking the bus or cooking a meal.
6. Encouraging productive thinking patterns through such things as education about the nature of the disorder, using positive self-talk and imagery, or examining faulty assumptions about self and others.
7. Increasing client awareness of feelings, thoughts, and behaviors and their interrelationship through such methods as ex-

ploring the relationship between family of origin issues and current behavior, commenting on here-and-now behavior in group therapy, and keeping journals.

Selecting and sequencing the appropriate interventions require a careful assessment of the client's current functional level, the manifestation of the specific disorder, and the specific situation of the client. Generally the more acute and/or regressed the client, the earlier in the list mental health professionals start. One way to conceptualize this strategy is to think of it as an "outside-in" approach. At first the provider and the client focus on external and environmental supports and interventions. At this stage the provider and other persons are mainly responsible for treating and supporting the client. Later the provider uses increasingly complex cognitive-behavioral-affective interventions in which the client is a more active agent. As the person improves, higher-order strategies and tactics become more appropriate. In addition, certain disorders are more likely to become chronic, involve a more severe regression, or affect feeling, thinking, and acting in different ways. Bipolar disorder is a chronic condition, but typically the individual regains his/her premorbid level of functioning once stabilized on medications. Contrast this with the often chronic and devastating progression of schizophrenia, where even basic skills are impaired. Or compare both of these disorders with the antisocial personality disorder where physiological involvement is a relatively minor issue but where cognitive distortions and disrupted family and social relationships predominate.

People are unique and bring their own strengths, weaknesses, and variations to the situation. A well-tuned treatment plan takes these into account. Some chronically mentally ill individuals, for example, no longer have involved family members. Family therapy is then irrelevant to the recovery of these clients. Or consider the person suffering with a borderline personality with a high intelligence who can bring rapid learning to bear in dealing with his/her incest-survivor issues. The client's individual strengths and weaknesses help to shape treatment.

A RECOVERY-BASED APPROACH FOR TREATING DUAL DIAGNOSIS INDIVIDUALS

Our general strategy for formulating a treatment approach for dual diagnosis clients is to blend recovery model notions with mental health ones. We first believe that the recovery model and the mental health model have many similarities that can serve to unite chemical dependency and mental health professionals and also can keep things simple for clients and their families. Table 1 contains selected comparisons between various aspects of recovery and mental health models. Inspection of this table demonstrates that many of the concepts are exactly the same or, after taking into account differences in language and emphasis, very similar. For example, both operate from a biopsychosocial model. Both look at genetic bases and disease processes, seek to modify attitudes and defenses, and emphasize the importance of social support and family involvement. Both models use many psychotherapy techniques. The A.A. slogan of "one day at a time" is a wonderful cognitive restructuring intervention. The mental health notion of attitudes following behavior is very compatible with the recovery notion of "fake it 'til you make it." Correcting chemical imbalances resulting from excessive alcohol use with nutritional supplements is conceptually similar to correcting such imbalances with lithium carbonate in bipolar disorders.

The two approaches can share the same general goal of recovery and can use an outside-in treatment strategy. The priority for early stages of recovery from chemical dependency is simply maintaining abstinence, and typically, the interventions rely on frequent A.A. meetings, calling sponsors, and looking at "stinkin thinkin" on cognitive attitudes signaling relapse. Later chemical dependency work relies on stepwork to achieve positive aspects of health through addressing issues such as guilt, fear, and resentment. Similarly, the priority in the early stages of recovery from psychiatric disorders is simply maintaining stability, and typically, interventions rely on case management, a structured life style, and acceptance of the need to manage the disorder. Later mental health work relies on skills training and psychotherapy to achieve positive functioning through addressing issues such as grief at having an illness, establishing intimacy, and operating as a prosocial member of society. We quite easily and comfortably say that the goal of treatment for our dual diagnosis clients is recovery from both disorders.

The two approaches can also complement each other. Education in the disease concept, stepwork, and involvement in A.A. require the ability to process information, to tolerate painful emotions, and to relate effectively to others. Knowledge of the neuropsychological impairment associated with different psychiatric disorders, ways to work with different psychological defenses, and behavioral skill training techniques to prompt prorecovery behavior can be invaluable in doing chemical dependency work with dual diagnosis clients. Those suffering from schizophrenia, for example, are especially im-

TABLE 1
Selected Comparisons of Recovery and Mental Health Models

Recovery Model	Mental Health Model
Disease process	Syndrome concept
Biopsychosocial/spiritual factors	Biopsychosocial factors
	Some attention to philosophical issues
Chronic condition	Chronic condition of many major disorders
Relapse issues	Relapse issues
Genetic/physiological component	Genetic/physiological component in many disorders
Chemical use primary	Psychiatric disorder primary
Out of control	Ineffective coping
Denial	Poor insight
Despair	Demoralization
Family issues	Family issues
Social stigma	Social stigma
Abstinence early goal	Stability early goal
Recovery long-term goal	Rehabilitation long-term goal
Powerlessness	Empowerment
No use of mood altering chemicals	Psychotropic meds used
Education about illness	Education about illness
Halfway houses, ALANO clubs	Group homes, day treatment
Sponsors	Case manager/therapist
A. A., Al-Anon, self-help groups	Support groups
Concrete action	Behavior change
Self-examination and acceptance	Awareness and insight
Label self as alcoholic/addict	See self as whole person with a disorder
Practice of communication and social skills	Practice of communication and social skills
Slogans, stories, affirmations	Positive self-talk, imagery
Stepwork	Psychotherapy
Use of spiritual concepts	Use of existential, transpersonal concepts
Family therapy	Family therapy
Group and individual work	Group and individual work
Continuum of care	Continuum of care
Nutrition, exercise, growth as value	Wellness concepts

25

paired in auditory–verbal information processing and benefit from more visual–motor modalities in lectures. Borderlines, typically survivors of traumatic childhood abuse, benefit from Step 4 work that focuses on current resentments and avoids dredging up of traumatic childhood memories. Providing anxiety-management skills to the client with an anxiety disorder can help insure that the client will get out of the house and to A.A. meetings.

Similarly, the recovery model can help fine tune mental health approaches to certain issues. Concern with preventing relapse is relevant not only to chemical use problems but also to such problems as noncompliance with medications or episodic cutting. The chemical dependency concept of enabling is also applicable to psychiatric disorders. Enabling occurs when significant others protect clients from the natural, negative consequences of their failure to responsibly manage their disorder. For example, families need to stop enabling those with chronic schizophrenia when they fail to take medication and deal with other self-care issues. The progressive structure and achievements of stepwork often give depressed persons a behavioral lift that they desperately need.

Blending recovery and mental health approaches does raise several controversial issues. These issues require resolution if the marriage is to work.

The first issue is the primary/secondary one, a distinction used in several different ways. As mentioned earlier, the traditional mental health view of chemical abuse and dependency holds that these problems are symptoms of an underlying psychiatric disorder. Although it acknowledges the need to manage withdrawal symptoms and other serious concomitants of the chemical use, this view holds that the psychiatric disorder is the "primary" target for treatment. People who meet the criteria for abuse but not dependency are especially likely to be treated within this framework. Similarly, the traditional chemical dependency view holds that the chemical involvement is the root of the individual's problems and that achieving abstinence and working a recovery program is all the person need do. Although it acknowledges the need to manage severe symptoms such as psychosis or self-harm with additional measures, this view holds that the client's chemical use must be the "primary" focus of treatment. People who demonstrate the more "subtle" signs of depression and anxiety are especially likely to be treated from within this framework.

Another way that professionals use the primary/secondary distinction is to prioritize the sequence of treatment. Although the psychiatric disorder or the chemical use is accepted as an independent problem, the most emergent problem requires "primary" attention. Only after a significant period of psychiatric stability or abstinence does the psychiatric disorder or chemical use or dependency merit treatment.

We stress the notion of *coexisting disorders and the need for simultaneous treatment.* We believe that some people who have problematic chemical involvement also have an independent psychiatric disorder. As we have seen in Chapter 1, a psychiatric disorder confers no "immunity" for chemical abuse and dependency and, in fact, appears to increase the risk for development of these difficulties. In addition, the synergistic effect of both sets of problems makes treating first one set of problems and attaining abstinence or psychiatric stability difficult. The provider must therefore manage and treat both problems simultaneously.

A corollary to this stance is the importance of a comprehensive assessment to establish that there are indeed two disorders. Given the manner in which problematic chemical involvement can produce difficulties that mimic a host of psychiatric disorders, and given the high case rates of chemical abuse in the general population and the even higher ones in psychiatric populations, the challenge for the provider is to establish the existence of the psychiatric disorder. For the purpose of differential diagnosis, a modified primary/secondary distinction is useful (16). At the same time, the provider must give equal weight to the chemical dependency *and* to the existing psychiatric disorder. Chapter 4 discusses these issues in more detail.

The use of medications, especially psychotropics, is another point of potential controversy. We absolutely refuse to recommend or condone the use of addictive medications after detoxification. The dangers of cross-addiction and the importance of a chemical-free lifestyle for dual diagnosis clients make this a crucial issue. But we are quite comfortable *using other psychotropic medications* after a comprehensive evaluation indicates that the client requires this for his/her psychiatric disorder. Medication helps the seriously mentally ill client become available for engaging in a recovery program, and the client's condition warrants such treatment. We do make sure that the client understands and works through the difference between appropriate medication and medications and substances with abuse potential, and, with less regressed clients, we encourage them to be honest with their own physicians about their problems with addiction. We also help clients to learn to handle any challenges to their medication use by a member of a Twelve Step support group.

The concept of the disease of chemical dependency and its associated concepts of the need to abstain and to accept the label of alcoholic or addict are also sources of controversy. Questions arise of whether some dual diagnosis individuals are "truly" chemically dependent (with signs of tolerance, withdrawal and/or loss of control) or merely abusers of chemicals. We prefer to use the term *chemically dependent* in a generous fashion with any dual diagnosis person who cannot say "no" because, as the research data presented in Chapter 1 demonstrate, chemical use of any kind is very likely to be problematic, escalating the symptoms of the psychiatric disorder and often adding its own set of difficulties.

Abstinence appears to be the necessary goal of treatment for dual diagnosis clients. The disease concept provides a nonjudgmental, easy-to-understand rationale for the need to abstain. The concept also helps dual diagnosis clients reframe their sense of self from being "bad" to being "sick" and reinforces education about their second disease or syndrome, the psychiatric disorder.

Some professionals see the insistence that the dual-diagnosis client label him -or herself as an alcoholic or addict as detrimental to the client's self-esteem. We would argue that the acceptance of the label and acknowledgment of this to self and others is therapeutic. We would also argue, incidentally, that this is valid for the psychiatric disorder as well. "My name is 'X' and I am an alcoholic and schizophrenic" is a statement in which the *label can be liberating*. Clients acceptance of their difficulties is a prerequisite for management of their disorder. Public acknowledgment of the situation also combats the denial of others and the stigma associated with these disorders.

The involvement of dual diagnosis clients in Alcoholics or Narcotics Anonymous and with a sponsor is sometimes a source of controversy. Concerns revolve around the ability of some dual diagnosis clients (for example, the individual with paranoid symptoms) to tolerate meetings. Other concerns include instances where an A.A. member has challenged the client's use of psychotropic medication or accused the client of not "working the program" when the client talks about his/her psychiatric symptoms.

We strongly urge our dual diagnosis clients *to attend self-help recovery groups*. These groups offer readily available, free social support that can help dual diagnosis clients with maintaining not only abstinence but also psychiatric stability. Moreover, these groups also help these individuals with problems such as social isolation, poor social skills, low rates of productive behavior, and distorted patterns of thinking that are associated with their disorders. Many A.A. and N.A. groups and sponsors are remarkably tolerant and accepting of the special issues and needs of dual diagnosis clients. We also do work with dually diagnosed individuals to prepare them for possible challenges to their mental health treatment and to enable them to tolerate the meeting process. We explain that A.A. and N.A. have no official stance on the use of medications and that a gentle response of "work your own program" is often all it takes. We will also hold mock meetings, go on trial runs to meetings, and coach our clients and their spouses to increase comfort levels. Finally, we help clients locate supportive meetings and sponsors or start such meetings.

Twelve Step work can also be a source of conflict. We employ *modified stepwork* with our dual diagnosis clients that takes into account the assets, liabilities, and processes that are part of the person's psychiatric disorder. Stepwork provides a standard, systematic approach that addresses key issues associated with problematic chemical use (17). As Chapters 5 and 6 explain in more detail, our experience is that dual diagnosis clients not only can do, and benefit from, stepwork for their chemical use issues but that there is also a positive "spillover" for their psychiatric disorder.

Many professionals have difficulty with the recovery concept of powerlessness. Much of their training has emphasized empowering the client by emphasizing strengths and assets. As we discussed earlier in this chapter in the review of Step 1 and its meaning, powerlessness and empowerment are not necessarily conflicting concepts. In working with dual diagnosis clients, our goal is to *empower them through surrender* by taking responsibility for their own thinking, emotions, and behavior. Powerlessness is a paradox in our view. By letting go of old, unsuccessful ways of controlling, undercontrolling and overcontrolling chemical use (and in some cases their psychiatric disorders), individuals can learn to relax, gain peace of mind, and begin to manage their disorders and live in a more productive fashion.

Spirituality is a final controversial issue. Phrases such as "power greater than ourselves" and "God as we understood Him" raise fears that this is an attempt to convert the dual diagnosis client to a particular religion or view of God. Members of A.A. and N.A. are very clear that this "Higher Power" is an individual choice and can be anyone or anything that could be a positive force in the individual's life. The concept is simply an attempt to assist the suffering alcoholic or addict to understand that (1) he/she is not alone; (2) there is help; (3) things will improve; and (4) will power alone will not stop the addictive behavior. These are valuable lessons for dealing with many psychiatric disorders as well.

Individuals with a thought disorder pose particular challenges when using "Higher Power" concepts. It is not uncommon for these individuals to have religious delusions where, for example, they believe that they alone hear the voice of God. We discourage discussions of Higher Power with someone with religious delusions, of course taking into account individual and cultural values when trying to determine if the person's notions are delusional. We employ a practical approach in which we keep discussions concrete and focus on having clients develop a sense of faith by looking at how things are better today than yesterday and how something or someone else can help.

We have even used stepwork as an intervention for certain psychiatric disorders and have had some success. Disorders characterized by impulsive acting out or rigid overcontrolling stances and by denial, rationalization, and projection seem to benefit from stepwork, especially the use of Step 1. Examples of such conditions include paranoid states with intact cognitive abilities and anger outbursts or assaultive behavior not caused by a neurological condition. Chapters 4 and 5 discuss some of these applications in more detail.

We should address one other controversial issue that is not necessarily part of the recovery model but is a common element in treatments of chemically dependent individuals (see Ref. 18). This is the question of whether confrontation is a useful therapy style with dual diagnosis individuals. A cardinal feature of chemical abuse and dependency is denial, a general term for a set of conscious and unconscious thinking patterns that minimize responsibility for the chemical use and the resulting difficulties. Putting clients in the ''hot seat'' is a phrase that gives the flavor of this approach for breaking through denial. Many professionals who work with individuals who are chronically mentally ill express strong reservations about the ability of these persons to tolerate and benefit from such confrontation (see Ref. 19). Instead these providers advocate a supportive approach.

We agree that, as a general rule, ''getting in the face'' of most dual diagnosis clients is counterproductive; in fact, we have witnessed one well-meaning counselor using confrontations who accelerated psychotic thinking in his dual diagnosis clients with schizophrenia. We would like to make some distinctions, however. As described in later chapters, dual diagnosis clients with antisocial features require confrontation. More importantly, gently commenting on the client's ''thinking errors'' (see Chapter 3) provides a way of holding him/her accountable without hitting the person over the head. Creating conditions of safety and commenting on process are ways that appear to work better than aggressive, content-oriented approaches for helping most dual diagnosis persons work through their denial.

Although stepwork is a prime focus of our treatment approach for the substance problems of our clients, we do utilize other adjunctive modalities. These include education about both disorders, family work, and skills training, among others. Wherever possible and within our overall framework of recovery from both disorders, we select interventions likely to impact both sets of difficulties.

Published reports of other dual diagnosis programs indicate similar stances on the controversial issues discussed above. Table 2 outlines these programs and their stance. Some descriptions explicitly stated the stance, some contained enough detail to refer their stance, and a few had uncertain positions on a given issue. The distinctive difference in our approach is the use of step work as part of our treatment.

EVALUATION DATA FOR DUAL DIAGNOSIS PROGRAMS

Published reports of dual diagnosis programs are few. Those with any outcome data are fewer still, and none have used relevant control groups and procedures. Two reports (20,21) indicate decreased days of hospitalization for program members. We have mailed surveys to post-discharge resources and asked them to rate the global improvement of the adults and adolescents with dual diagnosis whom we treated at 6 to 12 months after discharge. The professionals responsible for the care of these individuals rated 80% of them as improved or markedly improved. Obviously, however, more and better outcome research is needed. Until such research is available, the counselor or case manager must rely on his/her own judgment and on the consensus of others who have experience treating dually diagnosed persons to select and implement suitable treatment approaches.

PROGRAMMATIC INTEGRATION OF TREATMENT

The overall success of a dual diagnosis program depends heavily on effective organizational integration of treatment. Whether the program is being instituted on an inpatient unit or in an outpatient program, a clear structure and consistent philosophy must start at the administrative level. In the early stages of developing a dual diagnosis program, when either converting a traditional chemical dependency program to be dual diagnosis or implementing a dual diagnosis treatment on a psychiatric unit or in a mental health setting, it is essential to develop a clear philosophy and mission statement around which the program staff can organize.

Implementing the "coexisting disorders requiring simultaneous treatment" model requires a philosophy statement that is consistent with this theme. Administrative personnel need to speak, write, and demonstrate that this is the mission of their program. It is useful to establish a strong message at the start so that those members of the treatment team who aren't comfortable with that philosophy can either

TABLE 2
Program Stance on Key Issues of Published Reports of Dual-Diagnosis Programs

Program	Concurrent treatment	Psychotropic medications	Key issue Disease process abstinence labeling	A.A./N.A. involvement	Stepwork	Supportive approach
Sciacca (19)	Yes	Yes	Yes	Yes	No	Yes
Kofoed et al. (20)	Yes	Yes	Yes	Yes	No	Yes
Hellerstein and Mehaan (21)	Yes	Yes	No	Yes	No	?
Harrison et al. (22)	Yes	Yes	Yes	Partial	No	Yes
McCarthy and Byrne (23)	Yes	Yes	?	Yes	No	Yes

32

become more comfortable or chose another agency or facility to work in where there is a better philosophical and theoretical match.

An administrator or program director who gives an unclear or wishy-washy message will establish a climate for much professional and personal conflict among staff members. This is not to suggest that an overcontrolling stance needs to be taken by the individual in charge. Rather, the "boss" needs to give a consistent message about the mission of the program and to be a strong supporter of staff trying to carry out the program.

Physicians are key team members in a dual diagnosis program. In order to treat a client with coexisting psychiatric and substance-abuse problems effectively, it is imperative to have a psychiatrist who is comfortable with a coexisting disorders model. We emphasize the need for physicians who believe that both the disease of addiction and the mental illness require comprehensive, simultaneous care. We have found success when recruiting psychiatrists to be crystal clear about our philosophy and the mission of our program.

We have also found it helpful to have our physicians sign a "dual diagnosis treatment agreement" prior to involvement in any direct patient care. In this agreement we ask our physicians to agree to the following:

- No use of addictive substances after detox without prior approval of the Medical Director or equivalent
- Require attendance of patients at A.A. or N.A. meetings both during treatment and as part of the discharge plan
- Order psychological evaluations (including an MMPI) on all patients to insure a comprehensive assessment
- Require patient attendance in family therapy
- Not to discharge a patient until aftercare plans are complete
- Follow all rules of the program regarding urine drug screens, passes, visitation, level system, etc.

We have found that by making clear from the start all of our program expectations we create a more congenial atmosphere among treatment team members. Those individuals who tend to be uncomfortable with the treatment agreement have turned out to have a difficult time working with the rest of the treatment team. Therefore, the agreement serves two purposes: (1) it screens out anyone who is violently opposed to our philosophy, and (2) it makes clear our philosophy and mission to all team members prior to specific conflicts arising and provides a basis for resolving conflicts that do arise.

We would love to tell you that there is no difficulty finding open-minded individuals with fantastic clinical skills who have training and experience in working with psychiatric problems as well as with chemical dependency problems. However, it is not that easy. We have found that we can just as easily train a mental health professional to do chemical dependency counseling as we can train a chemical dependency counselor to work with psychiatric patients. We do prefer a recovering professional with experiential knowledge of recovery. However, the key issue is the individual and his/her attitude. It is important to find individuals who, like the physician, can accept the concept of coexisting disorders and simultaneous treatment.

We have found it particularly effective to have both recovering and nonrecovering individuals, and chemical dependency counselors and mental health clinicians on the staff to maintain a balance of approaches and to help cross-train each other. Staff members who do not believe in both the disease process of the psychiatric disorder and the disease process of the addiction tend to experience conflict with other team members and to be less effective in their clinical care of a dually diagnosed client. At a minimum, they are not helpful to the overall recovery of the client. At worst, they cause splitting and conflict between other treatment team members and the patient, and they undermine the recovery of the client.

Ongoing training is essential to the professional growth of all clinicians. This is a rapidly changing field. By the time you are reading this book there will be many new things discovered about treatment of the dually diagnosed population. Training assists us in sharpening our skills, validates what we know, offers us new suggestions, and provides an excellent vehicle for networking and professional support. In training new staff , we find it helpful to have them read the literature listed below:

- *Alcoholics Anonymous* (24).
- *Twelve Steps, Twelve Traditions* (25).
- *Under the Influence* (26).
- Selections from *Handbook of Abusable Drugs* (27).
- *Diagnostic and Statistical Manual of Mental Disorders—Third Edition—Revised* (28).
- Publications on the major mental disorders and psychotropic medications available from the National Institute of Mental Health (29).
- Selections from *Treatments of Psychiatric Disorders* (30).
- *Treating the Alcoholic: A Developmental Model of Recovery* (17).

Because of the high rates of dual diagnosis persons with antisocial personality disorder, with a history of incest, or with a history of being in abusive relationships, we also encourage our staff to read:

- *Inside the Criminal Mind* (31).
- *The Courage to Heal* (32).
- *Codependent No More* (33).

We also strongly encourage our staff to attend several A.A./N.A. meetings and to become familiar with the self-help groups in our area. We also hold weekly inservices on mental health and chemical dependency issues and their interaction.

We have used a number of ways to assure the quality of our treatment. A program dealing with a difficult client population and a sophisticated, blended dual diagnosis approach requires constant monitoring for quality and effectiveness. We use a scheduled review process by a special standing committee. We have found that involvement by key members representing both staff and management is important. Finally, having multiple data sources regarding the functioning of the program that include staff, patients, families, and other providers helps keep balance. We make use of satisfaction surveys to obtain these data.

ORGANIZATIONAL CHANGE

The bad news is that several years of work will be necessary to make all the changes in the educational, treatment, government, and other involved systems needed to meet the challenges posed by the dual diagnosis client. Interested providers will have to network with each other. Coalitions of providers, clients and their families, and key officials will have to develop and lobby for their agenda. This agenda must include changes in the training and certification of professionals, the reorganization of existing services and establishment of new ones, and the modification of eligibility rules and criteria for funding dual diagnosis care. The agenda must also include support for applied research, demonstration projects, and program evaluation studies. The good news is that this has already begun (see Ref. 34). "Double trouble" groups in Philadelphia provide A.A. meetings for clients with a psychiatric disorder. The State of Kentucky has offered several statewide dual diagnosis conferences organized by the Office of Mental Health. Comprehensive Psychiatric Clinics of Seattle has begun to offer an array of services for dual diagnosis clients. Rick Ries, M.D., and his colleagues at Harborview Medical Center and Hospital are conducting research studies of treatment approaches. We all have the same goal: cost-effective services for dual diagnosis clients and their families. We can join together around this goal, doing what we can for today and working for better treatment tomorrow.

REFERENCES

1. Miller, W. R. Controlled drinking: A history and critical review. *Journal of Studies on Alcohol, 44,* 68–83, 1983.
2. Institute of Medicine. Psychopathology related to alcohol abuse. In *Causes and Consequences of Alcohol Problems.* National Academy Press, Washington, D.C., pp. 133–151, 1987.
3. Khantzian, E. The self-medication hypothesis of addictive disorders: Focus on heroin and cocaine dependence. *American Journal of Psychiatry, 142,* 1259–1264, 1985.
4. Valliant, G. *The Natural History of Alcoholism.* Harvard University Press, Cambridge, MA, 1983.
5. Miller, W. R., and Hester, R. K. Treating the problem drinker: Modern approaches. In W. R. Miller (Ed.), *The Addictive Behaviors: Treatment of Alcoholism, Drug Abuse, Smoking and Obesity.* Pergamon; Oxford, pp. 11–141, 1980.
6. Miller, W. R., and Munoz, R. F. *How to Control Your Drinking,* second edition. University of New Mexico Press; Albuquerque, 1982.
7. Miller, W. R. Motivational interviewing with problem drinkers. *Behavior Psychotherapy, 14,* 441–448, 1983.
8. Schukit, M. A. *Drugs and Alcohol Abuse: A Clinical Guide to Diagnoses and Treatment.* Plenum, New York, 1984.
9. Kranzler, H. R., and Liebowitz, N. R. Anxiety and depression in substance a abuse. *Medical Clinics of North America, 72(3),* 867–885, 1988.
10. McLellan, A. T., Woody, G. E., and O'Brien, C. O. Development of psychiatric illness in drug abusers. *New England Journal of Medicine, 301(24),* 1310–1314, 1979.
11. Marlatt, G. A., and Gordon, J. R. (Eds.). *Relapse Prevention: Maintenance Strategies in the Treatment of Addictive Behaviors.* Guilford Press; New York, 1985.
12. Chick, J., Lloyd, G., and Crombie, E. Natural history and effect of minimal intervention in newly identified problem drinkers in a general hospital. In *Proceedings on Early Identification of the Problem Drinker.* National Institute of Alcohol Abuse and Alcoholism, Washington, D.C., 1980.
13. Miller, W. R. Motivation for treatment: A review with special emphasis on alcoholism. *Psychiatric Bulletin, 48(1),* 84–107, 1985.
14. Miller, W. R., and Joyce, M. A. Prediction of abstinence, controlled drinking and heavy drinking outcome following behavioral self-control training. *Journal of Consulting and Clinical Psychology, 41,* 773–775, 1979.

15. Marlatt, G. A. The controlled drinking controversy: A commentary. *American Psychologist, 38,* 1097–1110, 1983.
16. Schukit, M. A. Genetic and clinical implications of alcoholism and affective disorder. *American Journal of Psychiatry, 143(2),* 140–147, 1986.
17. Brown, S. *Treating the Alcoholic: A Developmental Model of Recovery.* John Wiley & Sons; New York, 1985.
18. Lowinsohn, J. H. Group psychotherapy with substance abusers and alcoholics. In H. I. Kaplan and B. J. Sadock (Eds.), *Comprehensive Group Psychotherapy, second ed.* Williams & Wilkins; Baltimore, 1982.
19. Sciacca, K. New initiatives in the treatment of the chronic patient with alcohol/substance abuse problems. *American Association for Partial Hospitalization Bulletin, 12,* 1, 1988.
20. Kofoed, L., Kania, J., Walsh, T., and Atkinson, R. M. Outpatient treatment of patients with substance abuse and co-existing psychiatric disorders. *American Journal of Psychiatry, 143 (7),* 867–872, 1986.
21. Hellerstein, D. J., and Meehan, B. Outpatient group therapy for schizophrenic substance abusers. *American Journal of Psychiatry, 144,* 1337–1339, 1987.
22. Harrison, P. A., Martin, J. A., Tuason, U. B., and Hoffman, N. G. Conjoint treatment of dual disorders. In A. Alterman (Ed.), *Substance Abuse and Psychopathology.* Plenum Press, New York, 1985.
23. McCarthy, K., and Byrne, A. Treating the substance abuser in a state psychiatric facility: Keeping it simple. *Occupational Therapy Forum, 4(33),* 13–15, 1989.
24. *Alcoholics Anonymous.* World Services, New York, 1976.
25. Alcoholics Anonymous. *Twelve Steps, Twelve Traditions.* World Services, New York, 1981.
26. Milam, J. R., and Ketcham, K. *Under the Influence.* Bantam Books; New York, 1981.
27. Blum, K. *Handbook of Abusable Drugs.* Gardner Press; New York, 1984.
28. American Psychiatric Association. *Diagnostic and Statistical Manual of Mental Disorders,* third edition, revised. American Psychiatric Association, Washington, D.C., 1987.
29. Department of Health and Human Services. Various publications. Alcohol, Drug Abuse and Mental Health Administration, Rockville, MD 20857.
30. American Psychiatric Association. *Treatments of Psychiatric Disorders,* Vols. 1–3. American Psychiatric Association; Washington, D.C., 1989.
31. Samenow, S. *Inside the Criminal Mind.* Times Books/Random House, New York, 1984.
32. Bass, E., and Davis, L. *The Courage to Heal.* Harper & Row, New York, 1988.
33. Beattie, M.*Codependent No More.* Harper/Hazelden; New York, 1987.
34. Brown, U. B., Ridgely, M. S., Pepper, B., et al. The dual crisis: Mental illness and substance abuse. *American Psychologist, 44(3),* 565–569, 1989.

3

Identifying Chemical
Dependency in the Dual
Diagnosis Client

In earlier chapters we discussed how care providers frequently serve
dual diagnosis clients. This chapter discusses some simple principles
and techniques for identifying the chemical dependency problems of
potential dual diagnosis clients. The discussion first covers basic
principles of identifying chemical dependency in general and then
examines the application of these principles to the dual diagnosis
person.

SCREENING

The clinician attempting to assess whether a person is chemically
dependent needs to keep in mind several important concepts. It is very
tempting to jump right in and start asking questions regarding the
amount of drugs and alcohol used. Remember, *quantity* of use is not
the basis for a diagnosis of chemical dependency. Rather, *quality* of use
is the prime consideration. The essential factor in making an accurate
assessment of chemical dependency, aside from physical dependence
as demonstrated through tolerance and withdrawal symptoms, is *loss
of control*. Is there an indication that the individual has been unsuccessful in controlling the use of drugs and alcohol? Specifics to look for
when evaluating for loss of control are:

39

- Did the person drink or use more than planned?
- Does the individual have rules about his/her use of chemicals such as "I only drink wine," "I only drink after 5:00 p.m.," "I never drink alone," "I can only have one drink per hour?"
- Does the individual ever break or dismiss his/her own rules about drinking?

Negative consequences are another indicator of chemical dependency. Father Martin, a famous priest in the addictions field, describes the criteria for identifying alcoholism simply as, "What causes problems is a problem." If drinking and drugging behavior are causing problems in someone's life and the individual keeps drinking and using drugs in spite of the problems, then that person has a problem with drugs and alcohol.

It is also important that an evaluator look at different areas of life function and any problems in these areas. Frequently these problems are a result of substance abuse. The evaluator should remember that the client is unlikely to draw a correlation between drinking and problems because of *denial*. (We discuss denial in detail later in this chapter.)

Social Problems

Social problems can be an early indicator of a drug or alcohol problem. Look for things like:

- change in friends (no longer associating with nonabusers)
- feeling uncomfortable in settings where no alcohol is served
- friends complaining about use of chemical or behavior associated with substance abuse
- inability to attend social gatherings without a "prefunction" (drugs or alcohol used prior to the function)
- feeling guilty over social behavior when drinking or using
- behavior when drinking or using that is not consistent with the value system of the individual
- sexual acting out when drinking or using, for example, promiscuity, having detrimental affairs, unusual sexual behavior, group sex, prostitution, etc.

Legal Problems

Many substance abusers find themselves with a host of legal problems. A history of any of the following may be an indicator of a drug or alcohol problem:

- arrest for driving under the influence
- reckless driving
- assault (nonfelony)
- solicitation (prostitution)
- burglary
- breaking and entering
- shoplifting
- drug trafficking or distribution
- driving with a suspended license

Adolescents typically have their own set of legal problems. These include:

- minor in possession
- breaking and entering
- burglary
- grand theft auto
- vandalism
- criminal mischief
- prostitution

Family Problems

Family conflict is an indicator of a drug and alcohol problem. Some providers have put the cart before the horse in always assuming that an individual drinks and uses chemicals because of family conflict. In reality, much of the family conflict can very often be a result of substance abuse. In other cases abuse exacerbates existing conflict.

One of the desired aspects of drugs and alcohol are the way they diminish feelings. However, genuine feelings are necessary for having an intimate relationship with another human being. A lack of emotional availability and honesty causes friction with loved ones, which builds into conflict and family squabbles. Things to look for are:

- increase in family conflict (not only with substance abuser but also between other non-drug-abusing family members)
- sexual problems with spouse
- avoiding contact with family members
- physical illness, depression, or acting out of other family members.

Medical Problems

There are many medical problems that are a direct result of substance abuse, some of which are very common to alcoholics and addicts.

Medical concerns that are often indicators of substance abuse include the following:

- sleep disturbances
- malnutrition
- hypertension
- gastritis
- ulcers
- heart disease
- intestinal difficulties
- emphysema
- diabetes or hypoglycemia
- hepatitis

Employment

For the gainfully employed substance abuser, the job is often the last area to be affected by drug or alcohol abuse. The alcoholic frequently holds the job up as an example of how drinking is not a problem. In addition, the income from employment is needed to continue providing funds for procuring alcohol and/or drugs. Indicators in the workplace that an individual may have a drug and/or alcohol problem include:

- difficulty in getting along with co-workers
- frequent medical problems and use of sick time
- Monday or Friday tardiness or absenteeism
- tardiness in general
- inconsistent performance
- labile, moody behavior
- oversensitivity to feedback or criticism by supervisor

DENIAL

Human beings avoid situations that cause conflict or emotional stress. All of us are familiar with the fight-or-flight response. Our instinct is to run away or engage in battle when faced with a threatening situation. Addiction is a *primary* urge. It is more important to the impaired user than food, shelter, love, or money. When the primary focus of your life is threatened, the natural flight-or-fight instinct takes over.

In the 20th century people do not usually club to death those who threaten their chemical use. Instead, they develop mental defenses that protect them *psychologically* from harm. A major defense is *denial*.

There are two forms of denial. One involves conscious lying, and one involves subconscious self-delusion. In the first form of denial one is aware of the lying behavior. For example, Jane says to Paul, "You've been drinking," after smelling alcohol on his breath. Paul, who realizes Jane smells the five beers he just drank, tries to cover up the fact with a lie and says, "No, you are mistaken." Paul is "denying" that he drank, but he is aware that he is not being truthful. In the second situation, Jane says to Paul "You act like you're drunk again. I think you're an alcoholic!" In hearing this information Paul feels that his ability to drink is threatened. If he really believes what Jane says then he will have to change his behavior. This would be difficult for him. Paul's psychological defenses come to the rescue. Paul quickly justifies his behavior, then switches to blaming Jane by responding, "Who wouldn't drink with a nagging wife like you. Besides, you think everybody is an alcoholic!" Paul is not consciously aware that he is "in denial." His rationalization is the way he flees from the danger threatening his primary urge to drink.

There are many "mistakes" in thinking that alcoholics develop in order to protect their drinking and/or using. Whenever the chemically dependent person engages in behavior that is against his own value system, he is forced to either (1) change his behavior or (2) change the way he thinks about the behavior. As the disease of addiction progresses, so do the mistakes or errors in thinking made by the alcoholic. Stanton Samenow, Ph.D., in his work with sociopaths (1), has developed a list of "thinking errors" commonly seen in the antisocial client. We have adapted Dr. Samenow's list for our work with alcoholics and addicts. We do not believe that alcoholics are criminals but, merely, that they develop a style of thinking that resembles antisocial attitudes as part of their denial system. The following is a list of common thinking errors experienced by both criminals and alcoholics. All of these thinking errors are forms of denial. The thinking errors of the alcoholic disappear once the alcoholic enters sobriety.

Alcoholic/Antisocial Thinking

1. *Excuse Making.* The alcoholic makes excuses for anything and everything. Whenever held accountable for drinking or using behavior, the alcoholic often gives excuses. Excuses are means of finding a reason to justify his behavior.

Example: "I drink because I'm depressed" or "I drink because my wife doesn't understand me."

2. *Blaming.* Blaming is an excuse not to solve a problem, and the alcoholic uses blaming to excuse his behavior and build up resentment toward someone else for "causing" whatever has happened.

Example: "I couldn't do it because he got in my way"; "The trouble with you is you're always looking at me in a critical way"; "My wife nags me too much about my drinking." Blaming permits buildup and gets the focus off the alcoholic and onto others.

3. *Redefining.* Redefining is shifting the focus of an issue to avoid solving a problem.

Example: Question—"Why did you violate your abstinence contract by
        drinking?"
        Answer—"I feel the language in the contract was too wordy
        and confusing."

The alcoholic uses redefining to get the focus off the subject in question. Redefining also indicates ineffective thinking, of not dealing with the problem at hand.

4. *Superoptimism.* "I think; therefore it is." The superoptimistic person decides that because he wants something to be a certain way, or thinks it will be a certain way, therefore, it is or will be. This permits a person to function according to what he/she wants rather than according to the facts of the situation.

Example: alcoholics will believe that they can stop drinking because they have made the decision to stop drinking, with no treatment or A.A. support. Superoptimistic people also believe that they can be famous, popular, strong, movie stars, rich, and so forth simply by wishing it and never take into account the practical steps along the way.

5. *Lying.* Lying is the most commonly known characteristic of alcoholic thinking. Most alcoholics lie in different ways at different times. They use lying to confuse, distort, and take the focus off their behavior. Lying takes three forms:

commission—making things up that are simply not true;

omission—saying partly what is so but leaving out major sections;

assent—making believe that one agrees with someone else or presenting or approving others' ideas in order to look good when, in fact, the person has no intention of going along with this or does not really agree. "You could say that" is an example of subtle lying by assent.

6. *Making Fools Of.* Alcoholics make fools of others by agreeing to do things and not following through, by saying things they do not mean, by setting others up to fight, by inviting frustrations and letting

people down, and in numerous other ways. By putting others down, the alcoholic takes the focus off his/her own behavior.

7. *Assuming.* The alcoholic spends a great deal of time assuming what others think, what others feel, what others are doing. He uses this assumption in service of whatever drinking or using activity or behavior he decides to engage in.

Example: the alcoholic assumes that other people do not like him. This gives him an excuse to blow up, be angry, or get drunk or stoned. Assuming takes place every day, and the alcoholic makes assumptions about whatever he wishes in order to support his alcoholic behavior.

8. *"I'm Unique."* The alcoholic believes that he is unique and special and that no one else is like him. So any information that is applied to other people simply doesn't effect him. Examples of these kinds of beliefs include: "I don't need anyone, and no one understands me anyway"; "No one can tell me what to do." Alcoholics in treatment commonly believe that everyone else is an alcoholic except themselves.

9. *Ingratiating.* The alcoholic often overdoes being nice to others and going out of his way to act interested in other people. The alcoholic is out to find out what he can get from other people, how he can manipulate them, use them, or control the situation to his own purpose. Watch out for praise from an alcoholic regarding your counseling skills!

10. *Fragmented Personality.* It is very common for the alcoholic to attend church on Sunday, get drunk on Tuesday afternoon, and then attend church again on Wednesday. To the alcoholic, there is no inconsistency in this behavior. He believes that he is a good person and is justified in whatever he does. His acts are seen as things that he deserves to do, or get, or own, or possess, or control. He never considers the inconsistency between these behaviors.

11. *Minimizing.* The alcoholic often minimizes his behavior and action by talking about it in such a way that it seems insignificant. He discounts the significance of his behavior. You will see minimizing when confronting the alcoholic about some irresponsible behavior.

Example: "I only drank three beers and I could have drank a lot more, but I didn't."

12. *Vagueness.* The alcoholic is typically unclear and nonspecific to avoid being pinned down on any particular issue. He uses words and phrases that are lacking in detail. This way he can look good to others but not commit himself to anything specific.

Example: Vague words include phrases such as: "I more or less think so"; "I guess"; "probably"; "maybe"; "I might"; "I'm not sure about this"; "it probably was"; "I drink socially"; "I smoke pot occasionally."

13. *Anger*. Anger is a primary emotion for the alcoholic. This is not real anger most of the time (in fact, 99% of the time). Instead, the alcoholic uses the "anger" to control others or to use power in a situation. The alcoholic has unrealistic expectations about the people in his world and controls others by aggression, attacking, criticizing, or any other way that he can to immobilize others, and give him control of the situation.

14. *Power Plays*. The alcoholic uses power plays whenever he isn't getting his way in a situation. This includes such things as walking out of a room during a disagreement, not completing a job that he agrees to do, refusing to listen or hear what someone else has to say, or organizing people to be angry at others in his support.

15. *Victim Playing*. This is a major role that the alcoholic takes. The underlying issues are aggression and power plays. However, the alcoholic acts as if he is unable to solve problems or do anything for himself. Alcoholics often whine, shuffle, look woebegone and helpless, and act as if they are too stupid to do anything for themselves. The alcoholic's belief is that if he does not get whatever he wants then he is the victim. Victim playing elicits criticism, rescue, or enabling behavior from those around him, while it avoids responsibility for one's own behavior.

16. *Drama/Excitement*. Because the alcoholic does not live a real life in the sense of getting his needs met directly, he often creates drama and excitement. Excitement is a distraction and keeps the focus off the alcoholic's own behavior and his drinking.

17. *Closed Channel*. The alcoholic is secretive and often closed-minded. The alcoholic needs to protect his drinking and using lifestyle. Therefore, when confronted with data about his behavior, he is close-minded and refuses to acknowledge the input, as it might jeopardize his continued drinking.

18. *Image*. The alcoholic's image of him or herself is important to maintain. Even a late-stage skid-row alcoholic will express concern at being seen at an A. A. meeting.

19. *Grandiosity*. Grandiosity is minimizing or maximizing the significance of an issue, and it is used to justify not solving a problem. *Example*: "I've spilled more booze than you drank"; "I can drink everyone under the table and drive them all home, so I'm not alcoholic."

20. *Intellectualizing*. Using academic, abstract, or theoretical discussions to avoid dealing with feelings or the real issues.

When trying to assess an individual it is important to recognize that person's denial system for what it is. It is not reasonable to assume that alcoholics or addicts are going to be open and honest with us about their use of chemicals. After all, we are threatening their *primary* need to drink and use. They are unable to be honest with us prior to treatment. However, when interviewing a client, if you notice heavy use of "thinking errors," this in itself may be an indication of a substance abuse problem. A dual diagnosis client will evidence thinking errors when he is using chemicals. Even a psychotic individual shows such denial in his/her response to questions about chemical use.

COLLATERAL CONTACTS

We cannot emphasize enough the need for collateral data. Obtaining collateral data is the best way to asses a person for chemical dependency. Given the self-deception and denial of substance abusers, you cannot rely exclusively on data provided to you by these individuals. You can ferret out the facts; but do not put too much stock in the alcoholic or addict's explanation of the situation. Family members, employers, court workers, physicians, and friends can all be an excellent source of information. Remember, however, that they too may suffer from denial, stemming either from their own need to deny the problem or from having listened too often to the excuses and explanations made by the chemically dependent person. Keep your questions to these people factually based. Ask, for example, "How many days a month is Paul calling in sick?" or "Has Paul ever been arrested before?" We should not expect others to have attributed specific behavior to the use of chemicals. Asking such questions as "Do you think Paul's an alcoholic?" may prove very unproductive.

ASSESSING CHEMICAL DEPENDENCY IN THE DUAL DIAGNOSIS CLIENT

If the average alcoholic has developed an elaborate denial system, then dually diagnosed individuals often suffer from twice the denial. Their world view is also impaired by mistakes in their thinking resulting from their own mental illness. The antisocial person has a triple dose of denial. The person suffering from paranoid schizophrenia is concerned about why you want to know these things and if you plan to tell "them" (whoever "they" are). The individual with a major depression feels so anxious, guilty, and worthless that he/she can't bear to face "all the bad things I've done."

In attempting to apply traditional chemical dependency assessment criteria there are special considerations that the evaluator needs to take into account. Dual diagnosis clients have several similarities in the pattern of their substance abuse to the "alcoholic-only" client.

1. *Loss of Control.* This symptom of chemical dependency is often clear in the dual diagnosis client. The problems the client experiences such as "poor impulse control" because of psychiatric problem are heightened greatly. The failure to drink or use consistently as planned is apparent in this population.

2. *Protecting Supply.* The dually diagnosed client is concerned about "having enough" to "do the job." It is common to find that he/she hides drugs and alcohol and has special stashes "just in case."

3. *Denial of Use.* This denial has already been discussed in some detail. The dual diagnosis client also tends to deny use or lie about how much or how often he/she uses drugs or drinks alcohol. These clients will evidence thinking errors.

4. *Consequences of Use.* Remember the "what causes a problem is a problem" definition of chemical dependency. The dual diagnosis client has more negative outcomes and instability in overall functioning because of drug and alcohol abuse than individuals with only a psychiatric disorder. Good collateral data are helpful in establishing the negative consequences of use.

5. *Systems Problems.* Many persons with a psychiatric disorder will show role dysfunction and problems with family and job. However, these persons often remain involved with family and friends and typically have routine contacts with various service providers. Dually diagnosed individuals often show heightened problems in their contacts with these systems and often have an increased frequency of contacts with the legal system.

Differences do exist. They include:

1. *Blackouts.* Accurate histories are difficult to glean from the dual diagnosis client. Blackouts and memory loss are difficult to ascertain when accompanied by a coexisting psychiatric disorder.

2. *Tolerance.* Change in tolerance is often difficult to track because of sporadic and binge use. In addition, the dual diagnosis client often is a poor historian, and the evaluator will often not have valid data to assess this area.

3. *Progression of Use.* Frequently the client's history of use is difficult to assess because of the problems described above. In addition, dual diagnosis clients often have limited capacity for honesty and psychological awareness.

4. *Withdrawal Symptoms.* When accompanied by a coexisting psychiatric disorder these symptoms of withdrawal can be masked by the psychiatric disorder. This is especially true of subtle withdrawal symptoms such as irritability, depression, and restlessness.

In clients with an already established psychiatric disorder, providers might want to suspect a chemical use problem when their clients demonstrate frequent episodes of escalating symptoms in the absence of obvious stressors or other potential reasons. Ongoing failure to comply with the treatment recommendations despite support and structure is another clue. Chemical use will often exacerbate those symptoms and problems associated with the psychiatric disorder that the chemicals can cause in individuals without a psychiatric disorder. Stimulants, for example, can cause psychosis in normal individuals. In our experience, the person with schizophrenia using stimulants (or marijuana) can demonstrate florid psychotic flareups even when taking antipsychotic medication. Alcohol can intensify acting out in psychiatric clients who already act out (2). Alcohol and other sedatives can often substantially increase anxiety and depression in psychiatric clients (3). In other cases, the substance use appears to mask the psychiatric illness. Some schizophrenics have reported to us, for example, that drinking helps reduce the "voices" (although others report drinking increases "voices").

In our experience, gross noncompliance with medication regimens, failure to attend day treatment or therapy appointments, or frequent hospitalizations, especially when the client signs out against medical advice, point to a possible chemical use problem. Watch for the development of problems in other clients when a new "difficult" client enters your services. This client may be giving drugs or even selling them to his or her "new" friends.

OTHER METHODS OF EVALUATING CHEMICAL USE AND DEPENDENCY

Research suggests that people will give more accurate self-reports of negative consequences related to chemical use and the frequency of use than of actual amounts that they have consumed. But this same research (and certainly clinical experience) suggests that self-report of use needs validation for all the reasons cited earlier in the chapter (4). Are there less fallible methods of assessing chemical use and dependency, ones easily accessible to most service providers?

Breath or urine analysis is fairly sensitive for alcohol use within the previous 24 hours. Urine analysis also has the advantage of being able to detect both alcohol and other drugs. This is an important consideration for the dual diagnosis population with its high rates of polysubstance abuse and use of street drugs sold as one substance but containing mixtures of other substances. Most psychoactive substances, with the exception of LSD and alcohol, can be detected up to 48 hours in urine. Chronic pot smokers will evidence THC in the urine for as long as 30 days. The increasing sophistication of certified laboratory procedures can, for example, detect attempts to fake negative UAs and determine whether over-the-counter cold remedies could account for a positive UA for stimulants.

Other physical tests are possible. High current blood levels of a psychoactive substance without signs of intoxication suggest tolerance. This implies chronic use of that substance or ones from the same family (cross-tolerance). A tolerance challenge is another assessment method. Administering phenobarbital, for example, with no subsequent signs of intoxication suggests chronic use of sedatives, hypnotics, or anxiolytics. Similarly, the administration of an opiate blocker such as naloxone will precipitate an acute withdrawal reaction in a person dependent on opiates. Readers can consult with medical personnel or the staff of their local medical laboratory for additional information about these tests. The problem with these tests is that they require a hospital setting, medical personnel, expensive procedures, and informed consent except in emergency situations.

A number of questionnaires exist that inquire directly about chemical use and use-related behavior. The Michigan Alcoholism Screening Test is a well-known inventory (5). The problem is that clients can fake answers to inventories. The developers of these inventories also had adults in mind when designing them. However, we do know of two self-report instruments that deal with the faking and adult-only issues. The Personal Experience Inventory (available from Western Psychological Corporation, Los Angeles, CA) targets adolescents and has items to detect faking. A relatively new instrument, this inventory appears to have good validity for detecting adolescent chemical use problems in outpatient settings. Its usefulness with dual diagnosis adolescents is uncertain at this time.

The Minnesota Multiphasic Inventory (MMPI; available from National Computer Systems, Minneapolis, MN) has both adolescent and adult norms and ways of detecting faking. The MacAndrews Scale, designed to detect alcohol problems, does a good job with "honest" alcoholics and a fair job even with alcoholics given instructions to fake good. The use of the Positive Malingering Scale (and a few other special scales) together with the MacAndrews does a good job of detecting alcoholics who are faking good (6). The validity of these scales for detecting abusers of other chemicals is not known. Our clinical experience suggests that these scales do detect polysubstance abuse. Another advantage of using the MMPI is the information this can give on possible coexisting psychiatric disorders (see Chapter 4). Readers interested in using the MMPI or other inventories in their work should consult with a psychologist.

The bottom line of this discussion is that, while methods other than a clinical interview are available that can identify substance use problems, they all have their limitations. These include questionable validity and appropriateness, especially for dual diagnosis adults and adolescents, and the higher cost of these procedures in terms of needing access to costly special technologies and experts who charge high fees. Obviously, multiple data sources are helpful, but there is no substitute for a good interview of both the client and collaterals. Remembering that any use of alcohol or drugs is likely to be contraindicated for a dual diagnosis client also makes the evaluator's job easier.

REFERENCES

1. Samenow, S. *Inside the Criminal Mind*. Times Books/Random House, New York, 1984.
2. Hesselbrock, M. N., Meyer, R. E., and Keener, J. J. Psychopathology in hospitalized alcoholics. *Archives of General Psychiatry, 42*, 1050–1055, 1985.
3. Kranzler, H. R., and Liebowitz, N. R. Anxiety and depression in substance abuse. *Medical Clinics of North America, 72(4)*, 867–885, 1988.
4. Leigh, G., and Skinner, H. A. Physiological assessment. In D. M. Donovan and G. A. Marlatt (Eds.), *Assessment of Addictive Behaviors*. Guilford Press, New York, 1988.
5. Seyler, M. C. The Michigan Alcoholism Screening Test: The quest for a new diagnostic instrument. *American Journal of Psychiatry, 127*, 1657–1658, 1971.
6. Otto, R. K., Long, A. R., Megaree, E. I., and Rosenblatt, A. I. Ability of alcoholics to escape detection by the MMPI. *Journal of Consulting and Clinical Psychology, 56,(3)*, 452–457, 1988.

4

Assessing the Psychiatric Disorder

This chapter presents a general discussion of some of the issues, principles, and procedures pertinent to establishing the psychiatric diagnosis of the dual diagnosis client. No substitute for the extensive training and supervision required to master the slippery art of psychiatric diagnosis, the chapter does provide an introductory orientation to special concerns of dual diagnosis, psychiatric assessment and emphasizes the pragmatic issues facing the average field worker. We urge readers to obtain consultation when attempting to go beyond a provisional assessment and diagnosis. Later chapters describe specific signs and symptoms associated with major diagnostic categories.

ISSUES IN IDENTIFYING THE PSYCHIATRIC DISORDER

Achieving accurate psychiatric diagnoses requires a comprehensive assessment to document distress and disability as a result of a biological or psychological cause. It is important to assess two domains. The first is the *intrapersonal* domain. A useful general way to think about this domain is to think of the individual as composed of three separate response systems, specifically the feeling, thinking, and behaving systems. The second domain is the *interpersonal*. This includes both quality and quantity of relationships with significant others as well as the adequacy of functioning in the areas of job or school performance, parent or child responsibilities, and leisure and recreational activities.

Another cardinal rule of psychiatric diagnosis is the absolute necessity of a good *history*. Never, ever diagnose using information based only on the client's presentation at the time of assessment. Without a good history to establish the duration and probable cause of the disorder, grave errors are possible. Finally, the provider should be comfortable making *multiple diagnoses* and, in fact, research has demonstrated that many psychiatric clients will have more than one diagnosis (1). The convention is to list first the condition responsible for the evaluation or admission to clinical care. Do not let this convention, however, sway you from the coexisting disorders model.

Establishing the psychiatric diagnosis of the dual diagnosis client requires respect for the special issues surrounding the assessment of substance abuse and coexisting disorders as well as the investment of greater than usual time and energy. We first need to consider base-rate issues. Epidemiological studies of general community samples, using trained research assistants and standardized interviews, have demonstrated that chemical abuse and dependency are among the most common disorders experienced by members of the adult population in the previous 6 months (2). Six-month prevalence rates were 5% for alcohol abuse/dependency and 2% for drug abuse/dependency with a combined figure (because of overlap) of 6.4%. This compares to a ratio of 1% for schizophrenia and 5.2% for affective disorders. Rates of alcohol and drug abuse/dependency diagnosis were especially high for both males and for females between the ages of 18 and 24. Phobias, major depression, dysthymia, and obsessive-compulsive disorder were the four most common diagnoses for older females. However, drug abuse/dependence and, most especially, alcohol abuse/dependence were among the most common diagnoses for the older males. Given the importance of denial, the use of urine drug screens and a careful look at prescription drug abuse might have yielded even higher rates of problematic chemical use in the general population. At the same time, approximately 20% to 40% of those meeting criteria for substance abuse or dependency problems in the past 6 months meet the criteria for a coexisting psychiatric disorder (2).

Rates of substance abuse and dependence are even higher in various treatment settings. Studies indicate that clients with substance use problems can account for half of emergency room visits; 30% to 50% of admissions to Veterans Administration hospitals and public psychiatric hospitals, and 30% to 50% of patients in private psychiatric hospitals (3). One study of chronic psychiatric outpatients found that only 27% had little or no substance abuse history (4). Conversations with providers in other systems such as the justice system and child protective services suggest rates as high or higher.

The implications of these data are straightforward. Given no other data about a person presenting for an assessment with emotional, mental, or behavioral problems, the evaluator's best guess is that chemical abuse or dependency is at least one of the person's diagnoses, if not the only one. This would appear especially to be the case if there is a history of treatment contacts or if the person is young or male. This, plus studies that suggest frequent underdiagnosising of substance abuse by clinicians (see Refs.5,6), suggest that evaluators always need to keep substance abuse in mind as a diagnostic rule-out.

Another key point to keep in mind is that persons abusing or dependent on chemicals can evidence symptoms that mimic a host of psychiatric disorders. Psychiatric syndromes can also frequently affect substance abusers. This can occur not only during withdrawal from alcohol and other central nervous system depressants but also during acute intoxication from stimulants, hallucinogens, and other substances (3). Studies have reported that almost half of alcoholics report a history of transient psychotic-like symptoms, that up to 10% develop chronic auditory hallucinations, and that, using more recent, stricter criteria for diagnosing schizophrenia, many alcoholics had been mistakenly diagnosed as having schizophrenia (7). Individuals abusing alcohol, opiates, sedative-hypnotics, and certain of the inhalants often show neuropsychological impairments and a variety of organic mental disorders including dementia (8).

In addition to substance abuse and dependence disorders, the epidemiological studies discussed above indicate that depression and certain anxiety disorders are common in the general population. Rates are even higher among individuals with chemical use problems. Rates of major depression and certain anxiety disorders vary depending on the population and criteria used, but rates range from 10% to 75% in various studies of individuals seeking treatment for substance abuse. Experimental studies of normal and clinical populations also show that low dosage and/or brief use of a variety of substances has positive effects on mood but that higher dosages and more extended use dramatically increase depression and anxiety as well as irritability and mood swings. Gender differences are significant, with more females than males abusing substances having concurrent symptoms of depression and phobia (3,9–12).

Data on concurrent signs of most personality disorders are generally lacking. The one exception is antisocial personality disorder and its associated traits, such as self-centered, impulsive behavior and asocial acting out. These traits appear to be more common among those abusing substances, especially illegal ones. These traits are also more common among males abusing substances than among females with substance abuse problems. Rates of significant levels of antisocial features in several studies have ranged from 5% to 20% for males and 5% for females in residential chemical dependency centers to 50% for males and 20% for females in inpatient settings (3,7,13).

Yet these same studies show that, in the majority of cases, the concurrent psychiatric symptoms disappear with abstinence and time. Evaluators need to keep in mind that the "psychiatric" symptoms of their substance abusing clients may be due only to the chemical use and its consequences.

Studies using the diagnostic principles discussed in the next section have demonstrated, however, that some individuals do indeed have independent, coexisting dual disorders. Estimates also vary depending on the presenting problem (chemical abuse/dependency or psychiatric disorder), the setting (inpatient or outpatient), and gender (male or female). At least half of all hospitalized persons with schizophrenia, for example, and 20% of persons with bipolar disorders appear to have a coexisting chemical abuse or dependency problem (see Ref.3). Among hospitalized alcoholics in one study, 14% of females and 7% of males had a coexisting phobia, and 5% of females and 3% of males had a panic disorder (13). Careful reviews suggest that 10% to 15% of individuals with a major depression and 60% to 80% of persons with an antisocial personality disorder have a coexisting substance abuse or dependency problem (9).

A comprehensive dual diagnosis assessment will take more work. Typically an evaluator asks probing questions in each domain of intra- and interpersonal function, and, if there seems to be a difficulty, explores that area in more depth. By definition the client with potentially two diagnoses has at least two areas to explore in depth. In addition, psychotic thinking disturbances, flash floods of strong or bizarre emotions, and other psychiatric symptoms make for a longer interview requiring constant effort to keep the evaluation on track and to elicit as much good data as possible. In addition, dual diagnosis clients are often unreliable historians and confirmation with collaterals is typically necessary. Even if the client is willing to sign releases for information, collecting information from collaterals takes time and energy.

In summary, an evaluator relying solely on reports and observations of signs of a psychiatric disorder when the individual has been abusing substances can overdiagnose a coexisting psychiatric disorder. None-theless, some individuals will have coexisting disorders and deter-mining this will take extra effort. It also involves using the principles discussed in the next section.

DIAGNOSTIC PRINCIPLES

How do we go about establishing that the client may have a psychiatric diagnosis in addition to a chemical dependency problem? In many cases a well-documented history or a clear-cut client presentation leaves no doubt regarding a coexisting psychiatric disorder. In our experience we have found six decision rules (three major ones and three adjunct ones) useful in thinking through the data gleaned from the client's presentation and history when the picture is less clear.

The first major rule is straightforward in principle. If the client's history indicates that the psychiatric difficulties began prior to the problematic chemical involvement (defined as heavy use and/or negative consequences), then consider the client a dual diagnosis client. While the coexisting disorders model is better for treatment purposes, this primary/secondary distinction is useful for differential diagnosis (14).

For example, one adolescent male presented with out-of-control behavior and extensive stimulant involvement. The history, gained not only from the boy but also from the divorced mother and the school, indicated that he had first become extremely moody and sullen while a student in junior high school, had withdrawn from any friends, and had begun to get failing grades at the time of the parents' first talk of divorce. Several times the mother had awakened to find her son sleeping on the floor of the soon-to-separate parents' bedroom. After the divorce the boy had gained a great deal of weight and had used diet pills in an attempt to lose the weight and not be a "fatty." The use of stimulants had then acquired a life of its own and compounded the original problems. The provisional diagnosis included both stimulant abuse and major depression.

In contrast, an assessment of an adult male with a history of being diagnosed as "schizophrenic" and of having problems with polysubstance abuse revealed that the voices had started after a period of prolonged drug abuse. This plus other data (e.g., the voices started at age 31; the client heard the voices as coming from *inside his head* instead of outside; and he had a history of multiple girlfriends) suggested that the voices were probably caused by the chemicals and were not related to schizophrenia.

This decision rule, although straightforward in principle, can be tricky to implement because of difficulties in establishing a reliable history. The client may be unable or unwilling to give a coherent history for a variety of reasons. Using a collateral and emphasizing not individual symptoms but the age at which the individual met all criteria for a disorder may help here (15). However, this does not resolve all difficulties. In the case of an adolescent the parents may not know when their child began using chemicals. Many clients also have a history of chemical involvement from early adolescence or even before. Because many psychiatric disorders typically have an onset in late adolescence or early adulthood (15), the application of this rule becomes problematic.

The second major rule is that the symptoms and problems that the client presents are qualitatively different than usually seen with only problematic chemical involvement. These differences can include the intensity, frequency, or pattern of problems. Compared to individuals with drug-induced psychosis (16), persons with both schizophrenia and substance abuse/dependency are likely to show more classical signs of schizophrenia (e.g., poor insight, disorganized thoughts, flat, blunted, or inappropriate affect), fewer signs of an organic mental disorder (e.g., disorientation, confusion, memory deficits, visual/ tactile hallucinations); and longer duration of the psychosis prior to treatment contact (6 months). Compared to male alcoholics (13,14), persons with both substance abuse and antisocial personality demonstrated an earlier onset of both social difficulties and use of chemicals, a pattern of intense polysubstance abuse with rapid progression, and more legal system involvement. In our experience the substance abusing patient who appears acutely manic when the chemical of choice is not a stimulant generally does have a bipolar disorder.

Unfortunately, using this rule requires experience with a range of treatment populations to develop that "gut" feel that can assist in the application of this principle. And the most common coexisting disorders of major depression and certain of the anxiety disorders such as panic attacks are very difficult to distinguish from similar symptoms caused by chemical usage (11,17).

The third major rule is in some ways the best and in some ways the most controversial. Namely, if the psychiatric problems continue during a chemical-free interval of 4 weeks after detox, then consider a second diagnosis. The period of abstinence can be determined either by information on the client's history or during a period of ongoing treatment and observation. The alcoholic for example, with 10 months of sobriety who develops panic attacks probably "really" does have panic attacks. Or a patient, abstinent as part of a 1-year stint in a cult prohibiting chemical use, but who continued labile, self-harmful, and erratic, is likely "really" to be suffering from a borderline personality disorder. A period of abstinence of sufficient length usually removes the chemical involvement as a confounding factor. A few patients do show chronic symptoms apparently caused by just the chemical use (see Chapter 5) but generally this rule works well.

The controversial aspect involves the length of time that the client must be abstinent to as certain that the client was not still toxic and under the influence. Some authors feel that many months or perhaps even a year is necessary (18). We have chosen the 4-week criterion for a number of reasons. First, our medical lab consultants tell us that even the psychoactive ingredient of THC in marijuana, notorious for staying in the body for several weeks because of its affinity for storage in fat tissues, is no longer detectable in the urine of most chronic daily pot smokers after 30 days. Second, the results of electroencepalography (EEG) exams (19) and dexamethasone suppression tests (a measure of neuroendrocrine function)(20) return to normal after 30 days' abstinence. Third, research data and clinical experience indicate that many of the "psychiatric" symptoms caused by the chemical abuse will subside in this time period (7,11). This is true even in the case of withdrawal from benzodiazepines, notorious for being a drawn-out process (12). Finally, we feel the need to take some action in a timely fashion and are uncomfortable taking more than a month. This is the period of time that many clients stay in controlled residential or inpatient settings and where the likelihood of detecting lapses from abstinence is higher than in outpatient therapy or with clients not under a professional's care.

We never use alone the three adjunct rules that follow to establish the second diagnosis. But we do use them to confirm and support a "yes" decision based on the three major rules. We also use these adjunct rules as tiebreakers when the major rules produce a "maybe." The first adjunct rule is that the client has a family history that supports the psychiatric diagnosis under consideration. Research has indicated a genetic component to such diagnoses as schizophrenia, bipolar disorder, and some anxiety and depressive disorders (16,21) and, at least for depression and alcoholism, the independent genetic transmission of their two disorders (14). If the client has an uncle who was in a state hospital for 30 years because he was "crazy," our index of suspicion of possible schizophrenia increases. Clinical experience suggests that most borderline personality disorders and many antisocial personality disordered people come from extremely abusive or neglectful families, and this connection suggests a possible personality disorder.

The second adjunct rule is that the client has a history of multiple treatment failures in standard chemical dependency or mental health treatment programs. We base this rule on our clinical experience and the implications of the material in Chapter 1 on the difficulty these clients have staying in treatment and in not relapsing. These failures can include leaving before completion of treatment, substantial non-compliance with program rules or relapses during or afte. ureatment. Rather than view these difficulties as lack of motivation for recovery, we consider the possibility of a second diagnosis. We treated one woman, a gentle soul, who had undergone 10 treatment stints for chemical dependency in 8 years and who had always relapsed. Careful evaluation indicated that the patient had an encapsulated delusional system, probably the result of her mild alcohol dementia, that made her suspicious and frightened of strangers. Her A.A. meetings were a torment, and she quickly stopped going. We have also received appropriate referrals for clients who cut themselves during treatment for chemical dependency or who required a police escort from the treatment facility after severe acting out.

The third adjunct rule is the person's response to a trial of (nonaddictive) neuroleptic medication. Especially when psychological testing done several weeks after detox indicates a possible psychiatric disorder and the "psychiatric" symptoms continue, a positive patient response to a medication that treats a disorder gives support to the person's having that disorder. For example, one patient remained hyperactive and irritable after several weeks of abstinence in our program. Lithium carbonate produced marked improvement, and we made the presumptive diagnosis of a coexisting bipolar disorder.

TREATMENT DECISIONS

Establishing the psychiatric diagnosis fulfills the first part of our definition of dual diagnosis as involving coexisting disorders. A diagnosis should not only indicate the range of symptoms and problems that the client presents but also suggest treatment interventions likely to be beneficial. These interventions might include useful medications, psychotherapies, behavior management strategies, and social services required by the client and significant others. A diagnosis also provides a means of succinctly communicating the same information to other service providers and funding sources. But remember, too, that our definition of dual diagnosis stresses not only the presence of coexisting disorder but also the need for simultaneous treatment. This definition requires both the establishment of the two independent problems and an assessment that other services are necessary to supplement treatment for the chemical dependency.

Sometimes a functional or working diagnosis determines treatment disposition in acute or crisis situations, and the "true," "primary" diagnosis is irrelevant for the time being. The client experiencing an acute psychosis or intense suicidal or homicidal ideation, even if it has been caused only by chemical use, will require psychiatric management. Typically the care will involve the use of antipsychotic medication where indicated, placement in a secure environment with 24-hour nursing care, and the use of reality orientation and/or emotional support and limit-setting. The situation is analogous to the need to manage acute withdrawal symptoms medically. However, establishing whether or not a coexisting psychiatric disorder exists has important long-term consequences. It is one thing to stabilize the chemically induced "psychiatric" problem and then refer to a chemical dependency treatment program. It's another thing to decide that the person will need both chemical dependency services and mental health services for the foreseeable future.

In other cases the person may have an established but stable psychiatric disorder. Many people suffering from bipolar disease, for example, are well controlled on lithium and can benefit from a standard chemical dependency program. Many people also have "mild" cases of a disorder and can tolerate and benefit from typical programs treating the substance abuse or dependency disorder. Our general preference is to refer to a chemical dependency program whenever possible. The person will receive more focused attention to his/her currently acute chemical use problem. These programs are also less expensive and involve fewer restrictions on the client. However, certain situations demand dual diagnosis treatment containing both chemical dependency and mental health treatment components.

What situations would determine the need for dual diagnosis treatment? We can think of five sets of situations.

First, some psychiatric disorders seriously interfere with the client's ability to comprehend information and translate this into appropriate behavior. A person with schizophrenia, even when stable, can often have difficulty tracking and registering information and applying a general principle to specific situations. Individuals with severe major depression also have difficulty concentrating amid their preoccupation with their mental pain and lack the "oomph" to push for new behavior and keep up with more routine clients. The patient with personality disorders associated with acting-out defenses are likely to see information as attempts to control. They will spend more time embroiled in arguing back, forgetting group, or shifting the focus of the lecture onto other topics than carefully listening, reflecting, and resolving to behave in more functional ways.

Second, standard chemical dependency treatment, with its emphasis on group work, confrontation, and working through emotionally charged material, can lead to the intensification of symptoms of the psychiatric disorder unless intervention for the chemical use problem has been specialized to address psychiatric issues and unless other precautions have been taken. This is especially true, in our experience, for Twelve Step work. A client with a schizophrenic disorder, even when medicated, will often become increasingly psychotic when exposed to high levels of emotional expression in groups and to demands for performance on their written work. The person with brain damage will sometimes explode with the frustration of being unable to complete a detailed, written 20-page Step 1 in 3 days. Severely depressed individuals, already hopeless and helpless to the point of seeing suicide as a viable option, will often take a listing of the negative effects of their use not as a springboard for change but as the final straw. Borderline personality disordered clients will become suicidal as the Step 4 work uncovers the anger associated with their childhood sexual abuse. The person with severe social phobias will feel engulfed and trapped in group and focus on escape.

Third, dual diagnosis clients will often disrupt the routines and pace of a standard chemical dependency program. A person with mania talking too much and too often, or the person with posttraumatic disorder experiencing flashbacks, does little for the smooth flow of a lecture on the disease process. Staff will also spend inordinate amounts of time and energy attending to the dual diagnosis client, to the detriment of the other clients. We remember one person who had suffered brain damage who was blind, disinhibited, and concrete, referred to us mainly because the other clients of a chemical dependency outpatient program could not tolerate the way he went on and on and on once he began talking in group. Our therapists used a touch-on-the-knee cueing procedure to help this client check his behavior. Together with our norms of tolerance for special needs, this allowed the client to remain in groups without a revolt by the other members.

Fourth, many chemical dependency programs do not have the means to manage the psychiatric disorder. Sometimes no psychiatrist is available to manage medications. Or perhaps the facility is not secure enough to prevent the out-of-control adolescent from running away or the suicidal adult from throwing him/herself out of a window. No provider or program can be all things to all people, nor should it try.

Fifth is the availability of a dual diagnosis program using the coexisting, simultaneous treatment philosophy. We believe that dual diagnosis clients require a multimodal, integrated approach that combines both mental health and chemical dependency approaches for the simultaneous treatment of both disorders. Increasingly, such providers and programs exist. Where they do not, the provider either has to put together the best possible arrangement or initiate resource development in the area. One general strategy we have pursued is to find a chemical dependency program sympathetic to mental health issues that has involvement with a psychiatrist equally sympathetic to chemical dependency issues. We have also witnessed providers starting task forces, pursuing grants, seeking alliances with the "other" camp, or even starting their own programs with consultation. Although already overloaded providers may not relish the effort involved, in the long run, the efforts pay off in clients who actually require less time and energy as they get well. And anything less is likely to fail.

THE MENTAL STATUS EXAM

A well-conducted intake interview, exploring presenting problems and their history, is often enough to establish a psychiatric diagnosis. This is especially true if supplemented with information from collateral contacts. Many dual diagnosis clients have a history of involvement in the health, mental health, legal, or social service systems where observations and conclusions reached by trained, experienced service providers are available. These professionals can help establish the clinical picture. However, when a person is new to one of these systems, or when collateral data are unavailable, or when he/she appears acute, the need for more in-depth data gathering arises. In addition, both persons with a chemical dependency problem or with a psychiatric disorder will typically evidence difficulties in the interpersonal domain. The evaluator must often rely more on an assessment of the pattern of intrapersonal signs and symptoms to establish a coexisting psychiatric disorder.

The mental status exam is a systematic procedure for making observations of intrapersonal dysfunction useful for establishing the psychiatric disorder of a dual diagnosis client. Although it is no substitute for a good history, the mental status exam helps to insure a comprehensive evaluation of the client's feelings, thinking, and behavior. The exam also provides a means for bolstering assessment conclusions with specific observations that might suggest the need for further dual diagnosis evaluation and for communicating with other professionals. The next chapter lists specific signs and symptoms associated with key diagnoses.

The mental status exam covers the following areas:

1. Appearance and behavior. Look for poor or fastidious grooming, bizarre or deviant clothing, unusual or bizarre postures and mannerisms, facial expressions suggesting strong or unusual feelings.

2. Attitude toward interview. Look for suspicion, hostility, ingratiation, dependence.

3. Psychomotor activity. Look for restlessness and agitation or for retardation, that is, general slowing of movement or speech.

4. Affect and mood. Look for flat, blunted affect with minimal display of emotion; lability, or rapid shifts of feelings; or inappropriate affect, where feelings seem incongruent with the content of the conversation or the situation. Look for excessively sad, euphoric, anxious, or angry affects.

5. Speech and thought. Look for rambling, loose, illogical, unconnected, or pressured speech. Look for bizarre content or suicidal and homicidal thoughts.

6. Perceptual disturbances and hallucinations. Look for responses to nonexistent sounds, sights, persons, and so forth.

7. Orientation. Ask and check for ability to state time (day, week, month, year), place (location of interview, name of city, county, etc.), person (self and interviewer), and situation with accuracy.

8. Attention, concentration, and memory. Check for ability to count backwards by 7's from 100, to correctly repeat random strings of up to five to six digits forward and up to four to five backwards (have these written out beforehand); to repeat three unrelated objects or a new address and to recall these accurately after 5 minutes; to recall recent events that the interviewer can verify such as the current issues on the news or the waiting room setup; to recall remote events such as when certain historical events occurred or the names of the three presidents in office prior to the current president. Poor performance on these topics often suggests serious psychiatric difficulty. (Encourage depressed persons to try their best.)

9. Intelligence. Remembering to take education into account, look for high-level vocabulary or lack of one; look for concrete interpretations of proverbs after demonstrating to clients that you want them to state the meaning of the proverb in their own words.

10. Reliability, insight and judgment. Estimate the client's cognitive functioning, motivation, and honesty; whether the client's behavior in various situations is likely to lead to negative outcomes; whether the client has some sense of present difficulties, and what some reasonable solutions might be.

Also useful is asking the client to copy a simple figure (such as a four-dimensional box or cross) to assess visual–motor deficits, something that is often missed in a verbal interview. Readers interested in additional reading about the mental status exam should read the text by Strub and Black (22).

A critical part of any mental status exam is the evaluation of risk of harming self or others. The evaluator should always ask about suicidal (or self-harmful) and homicidal (or assaultive) thoughts and evaluate further if such thoughts are present. You should not worry that asking will put these thoughts into the client's head. Rather, you should worry if you do not ask. If such thoughts are present, the evaluator should inquire further about (1) frequency and intensity of the thoughts, (2) whether the client has a specific plan and access to the means to carry the plan out, and (3) whether the client has a history of such behavior. The best predictor of risk is a previous history of behavior harmful to self or others. A specific plan and access to means is also a risk indicator. Degree of hopelessness is a predictor of suicide. The risk further skyrockets if a psychiatric condition or alcohol/drug intoxication (current or in the future) impairs the client's judgment and impulse control.

You can consider antiharm contracts and perhaps increased outpatient contact to manage a low-risk client. The medium-risk client needs this, plus such measures as the certified removal of weapons from his/her possession and a 24-hour watch by family and friends. The high-risk client needs inpatient hospitalization or, if the situation is immediate, police involvement. Remember that the courts have recently decided that the duty to protect and warn other individuals when specific threats are made against them overrides the client's right of confidentiality. Check your state laws and your state professional organization regarding this issue.

Consultation with a colleague or supervisor is often very useful for dealing with clients at risk for legal professional reasons, not to mention personal ones. The colleague can help you think through the situation in a clearer fashion, support you emotionally, and serve as a witness. Documentation is also very important in order to communicate the situation to other professionals and, in the case of a law suit, support your side. Finally, remember that persons with schizophrenia commit suicide more often than people with a major depression.

A final word about whether the client is serious or "merely playing games." Our own personal policy is to treat all threats as serious. Guessing a client's "true" motivation is often not easy, and besides, even "game" players accidentally kill themselves, misjudging the distance of those rocks underneath the bridge or the timing of the police's arrival, or harm others.

ADVANCED DIAGNOSTIC TECHNIQUES

The technology of advanced psychiatric diagnosis, although rapidly evolving, remains relatively primitive compared to other fields of medicine. There is no blood test, for example, for schizophrenia. Many of the new techniques are expensive, experimental, and not readily accessible to the average service provider. Procedures such as the BEAM machine (a three-dimensional EEG analogous to a CAT scan and reportedly capable of pinpointing faulty physiological functioning in specific areas of the brain) are promising, but these are new and available in only a few medical centers.

We briefly discuss two accessible technologies. The dexamethasone suppression test (DST) can sometimes confirm the presence of a major depression with melancholic (endogenous) features likely to respond to antidepressant medication. Normal subjects typically show lower blood levels (suppression) of cortisol concentrations for at least 24 hours after taking dexamethasone in pill form. Melancholic depressives show, in contrast, an abnormally early escape from suppression. Chemical use and even poor fluid intake can produce erroneous results (23). Some studies (20,24) suggest that the results may be useful in identifying any coexisting major depression in substance abusers after several weeks of abstinence, but this needs additional research.

Psychological testing is another method commonly employed to evaluate a psychiatric disorder. Active use of psychoactive chemicals or withdrawal from such substances can also produce psychological test results that are invalid for establishing a coexisting disorder. We would never make a psychiatric diagnosis based solely on psychological testing unless we had a documented 4-week post detox drug-free period and a good history. However, we often will administer psychological testing to get a functional picture of the person's feeling, thinking, and behavior *while he is on chemicals* or during detox. We avoid a final diagnostic label but use the test results to pinpoint extremes of functioning that can be a focus of treatment or that must be taken into account in treatment. The care provider will benefit from knowing that the person is suicidally depressed; that the client's thinking is concrete; or that acting out is likely, even if this is the result of chemical use or withdrawal. The testing can also indicate diagnoses needing to be ruled out. Repeated testing over time with abstinence by the client can help to sort out the role of chemicals in producing the client's difficulties and can document progress (or lack thereof). A psychologist with an understanding of chemical dependency and dual diagnosis can be a valuable ally.

A FINAL WORD

Assessing dual-diagnosis clients is a challenge for providers. A sense of humility, a willingness to remain open to developments, and flexibility in planning are important. You do the best you can for your client. Providers should be willing to transfer or refer out clients if their status changes, to seek consultation, and to make additional efforts to collect new data and reassess the diagnosis.

Our intent in this chapter is to introduce the reader to some of the issues, principles, and techniques involved in making the psychiatric diagnosis of the dual diagnosis client. In the next chapter we discuss in more detail the specific signs and symptoms of the psychiatric diagnoses most commonly found among the dual diagnosis population, as well as the treatment approaches that we have found useful.

REFERENCES

1. Wolf, A. W., Schubert, D. S. P., Patterson, M. B., et al. Associations among psychiatric diagnoses. *J. Consulting and Clinical Psychology, 56(2)*, 292–294, 1988.
2. Meyers, J. K., Weissman, M. M., Tischler, G. L., et al. Six month prevalence of psychiatric disorders in three communities. *Archives of General Psychiatry, 4*, 959–967, 1984.
3. Galanter, M., Casteneda, R., and Ferman, J. Substance abuse among general psychiatric patients: Place of presentation, diagnosis and treatment. *American Journal of Drug and Alcohol Abuse, 14(2)*, 211–235, 1988.
4. Safer, D. J. Substance abuse by chronic adult patients. *Hospital and Community Psychiatry, 38(5)*, 511–514, 1987.
5. McCourt, W. F., Williams, A. F. and Shneider, L. Incidence of alcoholism in a state mental hospital. *Quarterly Journal of Studies on Alcoholism, 32(4)*, 1085–1088, 1971.
6. Ananth, J., Vandewater, S., Kamal, M., et al. Missed diagnosis of substance abuse in psychiatric patients. *Hospital and Community Psychiatry, 40(3)*, 297–299, 1989.
7. Nace, E. P. Alcoholism and other psychiatric disorders. In *The Treatment of Alcoholism.* Brunner/Mazel, New York, 1987.
8. Grant, I., and Reed, R. Neuropsychology of alcohol and drug abuse. In A. Alterman (Ed.), *Substance Abuse and Psychopathology.* Plenum Press, New York, 1985.
9. Schukit, M. A. Genetic and clinical implications of alcoholism and affective disorders. *American Journal of Psychiatry, 143(2)*, 140–147, 1986.

11. Leipman, M. R., Nirenberg, T. D., Porges, R. E., and Wartenberg, A. A. Depression associated with substance abuse. In O. G. Cameron (Ed.), *Presentations of Depression*. John Wiley & Sons, New York, 1987.

12. Kranzler, H. R., and Liebowitz, N. R. Anxiety and depression in substance abuse. *Medical Clinics of North America, 72(4),* 867–881, 1988.

13. Peyser, H. S. Alcoholism and clinical psychiatry. In S. E. Gitlow and H. S. Peyser (Eds.), *Alcoholism: A Practical Treatment Guide*. Gruen & Stratton; Philadelphia, 1988.

14. Hesselbrock, M. N., Meyer, R. E., and Kreener, J. J. Psychopathology in hospitalized alcoholics. *Archives of General Psychiatry, 42,* 1050–1055, 1985.

15. Schukit, M. A. The clinical implications of primary diagnostic groups among alcoholics. *Archives of General Psychiatry, 42,* 1043–1049, 1985.

16. Christie, K. A., Burke, J. D., Regier, D. A., et al. Epidemiological evidence of early onset of mental disorders and higher risk of drug abuse in young adults. *American Journal of Psychiatry, 145(8),* 971–975, 1988.

17. Tusuang, M. T., Simpson, J. C., and Kronfol, Z. Subtypes of drug abuse with psychosis. *Archives of General Psychiatry, 39,* 141–147, 1982.

18. Weissman, M. M., Pottenger, M., Kleber, H., et al. Symptom patterns in primary and secondary depression: A comparison of primary depressives with depressed opiate addicts, alcoholics and schizophrenics. *Archives of General Psychiatry, 34,* 854–862, 1977.

19. Mandel, W., and Milisanatos, N. Protracted alcohol withdrawal syndrome. Presented at the annual meeting of the Research Society on Alcoholism, Charleston, SC, May 29–June 1, 1985.

20. Struve, F. Clinical electroencephalography as an assessment method in psychiatric practice. In R. C. W. Hall, and T. P. Beresford (Eds.), *Handbook of Psychiatric Diagnostic Procedures, Vol. 2*. Spectrum Publications, Jamaica, NY, 1985.

21. Extein, I. C., Dackis, C. A., Gold, M. S., and Pottash, L. C. Depression in drug addicts and alcoholics. In I. C. Extein and M. S. Gold (Eds.), *Medical Mimics of Psychiatric Disorders*. American Psychiatric Press, Washington, D.C., 1986.

22. American Psychiatric Association. *Treatments of Psychiatric Disorders. A Task Force Report of the American Psychiatric Association*, Vols. 1–3. American Psychiatric Association, Washington, D.C., 1989.

23. Strub, R. L., and Black, F. W. *The Mental Status Exam in Neurology, second edition*. F. A. Davis, Philadelphia, 1985.

24. Carroll, B. J. Dexamethasone suppression test. In R. C. W. Hall and T. P. Beresford (Eds.), *Handbook of Psychiatric Diagnostic Procedures*. Spectrum Publications, Jamaica, NY, 1985.

25. Dackis, C. A., Pottash, A. L. C., Gold, M. S., and Annetto, W. The dexamethasone suppression test for major depression among opioid addicts. *American Journal of Psychiatry, 141,* 810–811, 1984.

5

Major Mental Disorders

This chapter focuses on intervening with the five major mental disorders that most frequently coexist with chemical dependency. These five are schizophrenia, bipolar disorder, major depression, anxiety disorders, and organic mental disorders. For each diagnosis we discuss the typical presenting symptoms and problems that individuals with these diagnoses evidence as well as typical patterns of chemical abuse and dependency. A caveat is in order here. We have seen clients with each diagnosis abuse the entire range of chemicals, and we are no longer surprised by "equal-opportunity" chemical abuse patterns in any client. Nonetheless, in our experience clients with certain diagnoses show certain preferences and styles of use that we will highlight. We also review general mental health treatment strategies for each diagnosis that we find helpful and devote extensive portions of our discussion to the counseling approach that, in our experience, is useful in helping these clients achieve recovery from chemical dependency. We especially focus on early stages of recovery. We have included examples of special step work for several of the diagnoses in Appendix 1. We are currently in the process of completing a book that focuses in more detail on step study counseling with the dually disordered client.

THE CLIENT WITH A SCHIZOPHRENIC DISORDER

A great challenge for the treatment professional is the person who suffers from schizophrenia who is chemically dependent. The cardinal features of schizophrenia are substantial impairment of the client's thought processes and the bizarre content of the thought. Symptoms need to be present for a minimum of 6 months to make the diagnosis of schizophrenia. The condition also tends to be chronic, with flareups in response to stress, failure to take medications, or chemical use. A person who suffers from schizophrenia and is abusing speed is a handful and, if listening to the voice of God, is a poor student for a lecture on the spiritual aspects of the Twelve Steps. Table 3 lists significant features of the schizophrenic disorder.

There are three key issues in managing the person with schizophrenia. The schizophrenic person must take medication regularly to control his psychotic symptoms. Trade names of some commonly used antipsychotic medications include Haldol®, Navane®, Prolixin®, Stelazine®, Thorazine®, Loxitane®, and Trilafon®. However, those persons with schizophrenia often stop taking their medications. Sometimes the side effects of the medication are uncomfortable. Individuals with schizophrenia can also be suspicious of the medication or remain unconvinced that they are ill. Or sometimes the person becomes so disorganized that nothing gets done in a routine fashion. The second issue is the need for persons with schizophrenia to perform activities of daily living, including eating, grooming, and attending scheduled events such as clinic appointments. Socialization activities are very important to combat their isolation and enrich their lives, as is skills training in various areas of living.

Remember that you are dealing with a brain disease that impairs thinking and that medication *and* abstinence are necessary to control the symptoms of schizophrenia. Until the medication is at adequate levels, use techniques such as a time out in the person's room or contacts that are brief to keep social stimulation low. Even with adequate medication, the person with schizophrenia can experience high levels of disorganizing stress when around other people, especially if these other persons are showing intense affect and are demanding high levels of performance that the person with schizophrenia cannot possibly deliver. Use a passive, friendly, low-key approach, minimizing high levels of confrontation, challenge, and criticism, and give feedback in a matter-of-fact style.

A few individuals will respond to just education about their dual illnesses with medication compliance and abstinence, but in our experience this is uncommon. Additional measures are often necessary. Other strategies involve the administration of medications by other persons (such as a residential home manager) or even once-a-week shots of long-lasting injectible medication. Some living situa-

TABLE 3
Schizophrenia

Feelings	Thinking	Behavior	Interpersonal relations and role functioning	Chemical use
Generally inappropriate or muted	Confusion	Disorganized	Withdrawn and isolated	Polysubstance abuse but will abuse chemicals (e.g., alcohol, pot) easily available
Sometimes depressed or angry or anxious	Difficulty concentrating	Decreased responsiveness to others	Poor role functioning	Less use of opiates, sedative–hypnotics
	Concrete and unable to generalize information	Eccentric	May be able to do low-pressure jobs not requiring public contact	
	Bizarre content, delusions	Poor grooming/ routine		
	Hallucinations			
	Greater impairment in auditory modalities			

tions may try to restrict access to chemicals, but this is often not successful.

Think structure, structure, structure. Written prompts such as checklists for activities of daily living and hour-by-hour time schedules are useful. Even with these aids, the person suffering from schizophrenia will benefit from supervision by a case manager who can remind, prompt, and assist him. Many people with schizophrenia will require on-the-spot supervision in a residential home placement or day-treatment program.

When stable, the schizophrenic person benefits from socialization activities. This helps to keep him/her oriented and involved with others and provide support for coping with his/her illness. Many persons with schizophrenia can also benefit from skills training and practice in such areas as taking the bus, balancing a checkbook, and preparing meals. Other useful training focuses on simple social skills such as carrying on a conversation and perhaps even on-job training for simple jobs that have a consistent routine and are not overly stressful.

Many persons with schizophrenia have trouble hearing new information and translating this into new behavior. Use lots of visual aids and attention-getting devices such as exaggerated emphasis with the voice, shifts of position, and numerous hand movements during classes. Throw away your step study audiotapes, as those require too much concentration for these people. Keep material simple and concrete and repeat it several times. Help the client apply new material to each specific situation. Use modeling to demonstrate the behavior and have the client role-play the behavior. Above all, keep it simple.

Families of dual diagnosis persons with schizophrenia benefit from education about both illnesses, the schizophrenia and the chemical abuse. They also require help setting realistic expectations for what the person with schizophrenia can do. Families must walk the fine line between making unrealistic demands and enabling the person with schizophrenia by rescuing him/her from the failure to stay abstinent and take his/her medications. Contingency plans around scenarios such as "What do I do when my son shows up drunk and psychotic on my door step?" are necessary. Ironically, the treatment team often has debates on these issues that mimic family responses and the astute counselor can use these as a guideline for intervening with the family. Families also benefit from referral to support groups such as the Alliance for the Mentally Ill.

In our experience inpatient hospitalization is usually necessary to stabilize the schizophrenia and begin recovery. Managing acute psychosis and maintaining early abstinence is often impossible on an outpatient basis. A comprehensive outpatient continuing care program following inpatient care is also imperative for long-term success.

Doing a comprehensive chemical dependency assessment with someone who is psychotic can be a waste of time. Your best bet is to interview significant others (especially case managers) and ask if the client uses any type of drug or alcohol. Studies suggest that patients with schizophrenia use more stimulants, cannabis, hallucinogenics, inhalants, caffeine, and tobacco and less alcohol, opiates, and sedative-hypnotics than other psychotic patients or control subjects (1). In our experience, rates of both alcohol and marijuana use are high, apparently because these are easily accessible. Heavy use of narcotics appears less common because most persons with schizophrenia are too impaired to steal stereos, fence them, and cut a deal with the local heroin dealer.

If there is any report of chemical use, even "just" alcohol or marijuana, the person may need dual diagnosis treatment especially if the person does not remain abstinent after instructions to avoid chemicals. Any use of alcohol and drugs is contraindicated for the person with schizophrenia. Marijuana is a real problem. Our own clinical experience suggests that persons with schizophrenia who smoke marijuana, even when taking proper doses of medication, often experience a psychotic episode. When abusing alcohol schizophrenics tend to discontinue their medications since the alcohol further disorganizes them and exacerbates side effects of the medication. We do encourage the use of decaffeinated beverages and, much later in recover, the cessation of smoking. We have periodic debates with ourselves about this stance on smoking but generally conclude that abstinence from substances with more immediate negative consequences is a priority.

These patients sometimes abuse their side-effect medication because of the "buzz" that anticholinergic agents such as Artane® can deliver. Watch out for those clients who run out of their side-effect medication before their antipsychotic medication. They could be using (or selling) the anticholinergic medication. Some psychiatrists also prescribe a potentially addictive antianxiety agent such as Valium® or Xanax® for decreasing the schizophrenic's agitation. This should generally be avoided when working with the dually diagnosed person with schizophrenia because of cross-tolerance, cross-dependence, and the highly addictive nature of benzodiazepines.

Persons with schizophrenia often have strong denial about the effects of alcohol and drugs on their lives, not unlike other drug and alcohol abusers. However, pounding on their denial through heavy confrontation is not appropriate. Strong confrontation will lead to further exacerbation of psychotic symptoms. Instead, the task of the recovery counselor is slowly and painfully to build into the patient's world view that he/she is chemically dependent and cannot use drugs or alcohol, at all, ever, under any circumstances. Explaining that chemical dependency is a disease helps give schizophrenics a clear and concrete rationale why *no* use of chemicals is necessary, as they suffer from the disease of chemical dependency. If we can convince the person with schizophrenia that he/she is chemically dependent and that he/she needs to be abstinent, we are satisfied with our work. We do not expect him/her to complete the first Five Steps in the first 30 days of sobriety. We have modified our step work for this client. Our Step 1 focuses on unmanageability. We are clear and concrete. We stay away from too much emphasis on powerlessness as this can lead to further disorganization in the thinking of this population (see Appendix 1 for an example of step work for persons with schizophrenia).

We often ask clients suffering from schizophrenia to develop two sets of cue cards as part of their Step 1 work. We first educate them about the differences between needed medications (good drugs) and bad drugs (such as marijuana). We then assist them to write out three reasons why they need to take their medications and three reasons why they cannot use drugs. Often these reasons are very basic, such as "I'll end up in hospitals like this" or "I'll lose my housing." Checking with the referral source or case manager will help generate valid pertinent reasons. We ask the persons with schizophrenia to write these reasons on the cue cards and then to carry these cards. Our staff frequently ask them to state three reasons for needing to take medications and to state three reasons why they should stop using chemicals. We refer them back to the cards until the clients can state the reasons with minimal prompting. Using pictures of negative consequences cut out from magazines (e.g., jail) helps the less verbal person.

We encourage them to attend chemical dependency groups as soon as they show evidence of stabilized thinking. Often 72 hours of adequate doses of neuroleptic medication will begin to make a difference in their thinking. They benefit from repeated exposure to material and the support for abstinence they will find in a well-functioning group. Many persons with schizophrenia are slow to learn and require repetition of material. The counselor must also establish a norm of tolerance for unusual behavior in the group, especially a mixed group of people with different diagnoses, but also be ready to set limits and keep stimulation levels low. The counselor will need to supplement group work with a great deal of individual attention, especially if the person with schizophrenia continues to have difficulty in participating in a group format.

The person with schizophrenia most often benefits from a sympathetic A.A. group. The counselor should be familiar with A.A. groups that are more tolerant of medication use and unusual behavior. The counselor will also want to warn the person with schizophrenia that some individuals might question his/her use of medication and help him/her to develop and rehearse statements to rebut these comments. We suggest assisting the client to get a supportive A.A. sponsor who can meet with the counselor and the patient to discuss the medication issue. We also give the client the pamphlet on medications and their role in recovery published by A.A.

Do not expect miracles, but do not give up unnecessarily. Many persons with schizophrenia, especially with ongoing, comprehensive support services, stay abstinent and stable. Some, however, take two steps forward and one step back, but they do slowly progress on the road to recovery.

THE CLIENT WITH A BIPOLAR DISORDER

Bipolar disorder is a more recent term for manic depression. The cardinal feature of a bipolar disorder is a distinct period of extreme swings of mood and behavior ranging from manic euphoria and hyperactivity to depressed sadness and immobility. Some clients have only manic episodes but most will have a history of both kinds of swings or will go on to have both. In addition, some clients will appear for treatment during depressed episodes because they enjoy the highs too much or because the highs are only mild (hypomania) and do not lead to major difficulties. We are always careful to assess for hypomania in so-called "bipolar II" types. These people will have a history of two or more episodes of major depression and are only hypomanic in the interim. People with bipolar disease can often become psychotic and a not infrequent misdiagnosis is schizophrenia. In our experience, adolescents who are acting out can also be undiagnosed bipolars. The energy by which some antisocial adolescents propel themselves into trouble often turns out to be a manic episode that is treatable with lithium. Table 4 references key symptoms and problems for the manic phase, and Table 5 for the depressed phase.

People suffering from bipolar disease present three key treatment issues. First is medication compliance. Bipolar disorder is a disorder of brain chemistry and the drug *lithium* (sometimes supplemented by an

TABLE 4
Mania

Feeling	Thinking	Behavior	Interpersonal relations and role functioning	Chemical use
Euphoric, up, high	Grandiose, unrealistically optimistic	Hyperactive	Conflict with family, authority, anyone saying no	Polysubstance abuse and dependence, use of alcohol during highs
Sometimes irritable, angry, esp. when blocked	Racing thoughts	Decreased sleep	Decreased functioning during acute episodes	Use of stimulants during highs and lows
History of severe depression	Distractible	Flamboyant, loud, outrageous manner	Very often good functioning between episodes	
		Many projects, reckless activity		

TABLE 5
Major Depression

Feeling	Thinking	Behavior	Interpersonal relations and role functioning	Chemical use
Down, blue, sad	Diminished ability to concentrate, make decisions	Apathetic and slowed down, decreased activity	Withdrawn, isolated	Polysubstance abuse and dependency, heavy use of alcohol and other depressant drugs
Sometimes irritable	Helpless/hopeless mind set	May have decreased eating and sleeping, occasionally increased eating and sleeping	Decreased functioning between episodes	
	Guilty feelings	May be agitated		
	Thoughts of death and dying, self-harm	In some adolescents, acting out		
	May have delusions in severe cases			
	In some older clients, serious confusion			

antipsychotic during the acute phase) generally controls the symptoms very well. However, many bipolar clients like the highs (while they dread the lows) and often stop taking their medications. Another refrain we have heard is that they had been taking their medications, that they were doing just fine, and then decided that they did not need their medication! Finally, people on lithium require routine blood tests to ascertain blood levels and these can be annoying and can be a constant reminder of their "abnormality." Education about their illness and the need for medication is often effective in maintaining compliance, but some clients require case-management-type monitoring to help them stay on medications.

Another issue for persons with a bipolar disorder is their need for grief work. Many people stabilize only to find they have had multiple sexual encounters, spent all the family's money, and alienated everyone with their talk of calling the President and sharing a new idea they have for saving the United States. They need to accept their losses, repair and make amends where they can, and let go of the rest.

Periods of stress can trigger further manic–depressive episodes, even when the client is taking medication. The third issue is the need for a balanced lifestyle, with a reasonable mixture of work, play, love, and proper attention to nutrition and exercise is useful. Also helpful is client use of stress management and time management skills. The counselor can make these a focus of treatment once the client is stable.

If not angry and threatening, persons in a manic state can be fun to work with, but only for short periods. Their enthusiasm, energy, and giddy mood are infectious but ultimately tiring. As a general rule, we avoid any attempt to stop the manic behavior. Instead, we try to redirect the energy into such things as taking notes (often copious) during meetings or encouraging fast pacing up and down the hallway. Sometimes lowering stimulation levels with brief times out in their room or making sure there is no loud music is useful. We limit the client to 5 minutes air time in group per comment, permit no more than three air times a group, and require him to be seated. We establish hand signals or cue words with the client in order to get the client to slow down or terminate lengthy or rambling monologues.

Educating families about the illness, helping members deal with the family member's out-of-control behavior and referral to a support group is very often necessary. Living with a cyclone is not easy.

When the mania is very acute, hospitalization is necessary to stabilize behavior and insure initial abstinence. Intensive outpatient treatment can be quite effective in both initiating and maintaining sobriety in cases where the manic episode is not so acute. People with bipolar disease can also be treated successfully in a standard chemical dependency program if they have had at least several months of stability on lithium, or where psychiatric consultation is available and counseling staff are well versed in working with this population.

Individuals with bipolar disease have a strong tendency to abuse chemicals. Mania, like chemical dependency, is a good example of out-of-control behavior and the two together are a dynamite combination. These people abuse all kinds of chemicals but seem to show a special affinity for stimulants to keep the manic high going and alcohol to help them sleep (2). The fact that they accelerate their chemical use during the manic phase has led to the belief that these individuals are only self-medicating and that controlling the mania will eliminate the chemical use problem. We feel this is not always the case. We have seen numbers of people with bipolar disease who cannot stop abusing alcohol or drugs between episodes and whose failure to maintain abstinence contributes to another manic relapse.

We ask the person in manic phase to keep his responses to chemical dependency lectures and step work clear, concise, and as reality-based as possible. We respond with gentle but firm limit setting to such things as 50 written pages of run-on sentences, designations of themselves as the Higher Power, and attempts to rewrite the Twelve Steps. As lithium levels approach the therapeutic range, these individuals will become more and more workable. The recovery approach can help the client deal not only with their chemical dependency but also their bipolar illness. Both are diseases, both involve issues of out-of-control behavior, and both provide a way of doing grief work and repairing the personal and interpersonal damage associated with these diseases. Examples of step work specialized for the manic client can be found in Appendix 1.

We encourage our clients to get involved in A.A. as well as other Twelve Step support groups and to get a sponsor. We try to help structure these interactions so that the client learns boundaries and doesn't burn out a well-meaning sponsor with eight phone calls a day or monopolize A.A. meetings with lengthy rambling speeches on spirituality.

Persons with bipolar disease very often do well, maintaining abstinence and showing few residual deficits from their bipolar disorder.

THE CLIENT WITH A MAJOR DEPRESSIVE DISORDER

As we have seen in previous chapters, the majority of chemically dependent clients meet the criteria for major depression when abusing substances. Physiological depletion and a life increasingly out of control, littered with losses as well as frequent exposure to family role models who numbed feelings with chemicals, would make any person depressed (3). Abstinence and a recovery program typically result in alleviation of this depression. However, some clients also have a severe depression requiring additional attention, and at least one study demonstrated high rates of major depression among female inpatient alcoholics with an onset prior to active alcohol abuse (5). In some cases medication will be necessary. The guidelines discussed in Chapter 4 should help the reader sort out which clients are truly dual diagnosis.

The various subtypes of depression are another source of conflict. While all depressions share common characteristics, different subtypes require different treatment approaches. The cardinal feature of a major depression is a deep, lasting mood characterized by blue, sad, down feelings and accompanied by reduced rates of behavior and other symptoms and problems lasting at least 2 weeks. Major depression does not involve sadness because of the death of a loved one or a discrete, one-time response to a stressor such as losing a job. Table 5 outlines typical symptoms and problems associated with major depression.

One important subtype of major depression is the melancholic (endogenous) subtype. The DSM-III-R criteria (4) for the melancholic subtype include (1) loss of interest or pleasure in all or most activities; (2) lack of reactivity to usually pleasurable stimuli; (3) depression regularly worse in the morning; (4) early morning awakening; (5) observable psychomotor retardation (slowing) or agitation; (6) significant anorexia or weight loss; (7) no significant personality disturbance before the first episode; (8) one or more previous episodes with total or almost total recovery; and (9) previous good response to specific and adequate somatic antidepressant therapy. Five or more of these indicators suggest a melancholic depression with substantial physiological components that often respond to, and benefit from, medication or other medical-type interventions. One useful way of thinking about an endogenous depression is to make a distinction between biological (appetite, sleep, sex) and social reinforcers (fun activities, socializing, job or school performance). Melancholic depression involves the loss of positive reinforcing properties of both social *and* biological reinforcers.

Another significant subtype, as the criteria above suggest, is a major depression experienced by someone with a personality disorder. We describe this sort of depression as a "personality disorder in crisis." These depressions typically involve a strong cognitive component of hopelessness, poor morale, and suicidal ideation, and they represent the failure of longstanding ways of dealing with the world. The antisocial personality, for example, will sometimes experience a brief but profound depression when put in jail, something we call an "I got caught" depression. Although these depressions are legitimate and require management, the long-term focus needs to be the personality disorder and the treatment of choice is psychotherapy. Medication is generally not indicated. The next chapter presents a more extended discussion of certain personality disorders. Some depressions can even assume psychotic proportions and the various subtypes are not mutually exclusive. Careful observation and a thorough history are essential, especially when one is dealing with the depressed dual diagnosis client.

When a careful evaluation (including a good history, psychological evaluation, and a period of abstinence) indicates the presence of melancholic symptoms not caused by chemical use, the depressed client should be considered a candidate for antidepressant medication such as Elavil®, Norpramin®, or Parnate®. We are careful to avoid the antidepressants that have sedating qualities or that include antianxiety medication because of the potential for abuse. Psychiatrists familiar with dual diagnosis work have suggested that such antidepressant medications as Adapin®, Desyrel®, Limbitrol®, and Sinequan® have some abuse potential and clinicians report that they have encountered addicts who abuse these types of antidepressant medication. This is an issue needing more research. Always consult with a qualified psychiatrist regarding medication issues. We are also very, very conservative about the use of medications with adolescents. In general we find most adolescents can benefit from social–behavioral interventions. Some recent literature on cocaine addiction suggests that cocaine (and other stimulants) is uniquely potent in depleting the addict of key brain chemicals necessary to avoid a severe postdetox depression. These authors suggest that antidepressants are helpful, perhaps even necessary, for the recovery of the cocaine or crack abuser (see Ref. 6). This is a controversial issue and our general policy is to attempt a period of abstinence to assess the need for adjunct treatment. Keep in mind that medication can often take several weeks to affect the client's depression and support through this period is important.

Increasing the activity rate and decreasing negative thoughts of those suffering from depression are also important treatment objectives. We like to pinpoint potentially pleasant activities with people and help them engage in these activities. Contracting for the smallest activity they could possibly do and writing up daily and weekly schedules are helpful here. A discussion about the fact that a positive mood comes from doing pleasant or constructive activities can help challenge the faulty thinking of many depressed people that they need to feel good

before doing good. Making lists of positive attributes and accomplish-
ments and encouraging the client to engage in scheduled positive
self-talk sessions are other ways to combat the negative thinking
prevalent in major depression. The care provider can also gently
challenge the reality basis of cognitive distortions such as "It's all my
fault," "Nothing will ever be better," and "Things are grim and will
get worse." The assignment of behavioral "experiments" to test out
negative distortions often gets good results. For example, the clinician
could encourage the depressed person believing that no one likes him
to select a "former" friend to ask about that person's feelings toward
him or her. Try to pick a friend who still is a friend, however.

Building or rebuilding social support systems is a crucial component
of treatment for major depressives. Many persons with major depression have family conflicts, and individuals with good support systems
seem to weather stress and losses better than those with no one to turn
to for material and emotional support. Whether cause or effect or both,
an important target for treatment must often be the depressive's
impoverished and/or conflicted social support system. Many depressed people also demonstrate social skill deficits and benefit from
such interventions as assertion training.

We use a kind but firm approach with seriously depressed individuals and push for more healthy behavior. Gentle insistence is often
effective with this population, as is setting time limits for sessions of
complaints, "poor me's," and other unhelpful behavior. Keep in mind
that many seriously depressed people have trouble concentrating and
are more impaired in the visual–motor channels. Use auditory input,
ask them to give you summaries back, and be prepared to repeat
information. Auditory tapes are useful here.

Dual diagnosis persons with a major depression present a variety of
patterns of chemical use in our experience. We have noticed a heavy
use of sedatives, tranquilizers, and alcohol abuse in depressed clients.
Older individuals tend to abuse alcohol or antianxiety agents while
younger clients evidence more polysubstance use.

We have found it important not to be too quick to relieve the
depression of the chemically dependent client that stems from grief at
the losses caused by their use. This "grief" depression permits a
window through denial that allows the chemically dependent client to
see him/herself in a realistic manner. Step work and other components
of a good recovery program will help to resolve this grief. Needless to
say, abstinence is necessary for this to occur.

A moderately depressed person without melancholic symptoms who
is abusing chemicals may benefit from an exclusively chemical dependency approach. The support network provided by A.A., the reframe

provided by the disease concept (sick getting well, not bad getting good), the structured activities of Twelve Step work, and the practice of expressing feelings in a direct, honest manner can all be effective antidotes for depression.

Severe depression with either a high risk of suicide or melancholic symptoms requires a dual diagnosis approach. Management of the potential for suicide through contracting for safety, through mobilization of family and friends, or through hospitalization is required. Medication for melancholic symptoms is necessary. Education about the need for medication and finding A.A. groups sympathetic to medication usage are helpful.

We have not found it necessary to modify our Twelve Step work with the depressed person. We do, however, put a strong emphasis on strengths and assets and do not allow the individual to castigate himself over past behaviors. We may also augment our recovery work with referral to a psychiatrist with dual-diagnosis expertise for a medication evaluation and the involvement of a similarly experienced mental health professional for psychotherapy.

The chances of recovery for the depressed dual diagnosis client with appropriate treatment are excellent. The challenge for the treatment provider is determining the appropriate treatment and assuring that the client understands that he/she has two diseases—chemical dependency *and* depression. Abstinence alone will not remove the depression, and psychotherapy and antidepressants alone will not eliminate substance abuse.

THE CLIENT WITH AN ANXIETY DISORDER

The cardinal features of the anxiety disorders are anxious arousal and avoidance of the anxiety-provoking situation. Table 6 outlines additional features of this set of disorders. Under the general rubric of anxiety disorders fall a number of specific conditions: (1) panic disorder with or without agoraphobia; (2) agoraphobia; (3) social phobia; (4) simple phobia; (5) obsessive–compulsive disorder; (6) posttraumatic stress disorder; and (7) generalized anxiety disorder. Readers interested in the exact DSM-III-R (4) diagnostic criteria for each should refer to this publication. Generally though, a useful distinction for thinking about these disorders is the degree to which there is a specific focus to trigger the anxiety. These triggers can range from specific phobias (for example, fear of snakes) through agoraphobia (fear of being in places where escape is difficult or help not available) to the recurrent, out-of-the-blue panic attacks up to the

TABLE 6
Anxiety Disorders

Feeling	Thinking	Behavior	Interpersonal relations and role functioning	Chemical use
Tension fearfulness, discomfort Panic, fear	Worry Difficulty concentrating Flashbacks, intrusive thoughts Blocking of thoughts	Avoidance of feared situations Hypervigilance Bodily symptoms of tension	Withdrawal, isolation Detachment from others Decreased role functioning	Polysubstance abuse and dependence; some preference for alcohol and other sedative–hypnotics; may use cocaine in attempts to achieve euphoria

anxious-all-the-time feeling of generalized anxiety disorder. The more focused the trigger, the less incapacitating the disorder generally is for the client, and the more relevant are specific behavior interventions. As we have seen in earlier chapters, anxiety disorders (especially phobias) are common in the general population and among substance abusers. Abstinence will resolve the situation for many substance abusers, but a significant minority appear to have coexisting anxiety disorders (5,7). Again, a comprehensive evaluation to determine the existence of a coexisting anxiety disorder is necessary.

Not surprisingly, alcohol and the other sedative–hypnotics are commonly abused in this population. Individuals with severe anxiety use substances to seek relief, and this can start the abuse cycle. Taking a drink or tranquilizers "just in case" becomes behavior that reinforces avoidance as well. Medical personnel unfamiliar with dual diagnosis issues and given distorted information by addicted clients often prescribe antianxiety agents for individuals presenting with these disorders. This runs the risk of establishing an addiction, provoking relapse, or creating an additional addiction because of the cross-addictive qualities of these sets of chemicals. In addition, it promotes the false assumption that the cure to the distress lies outside of the patients themselves. Taking a pill to fix things can become an easy way to avoid work necessary to lead to long-term recovery. Instead, the focus generally needs to be on psychotherapeutic strategies.

Generally we like to teach the person with an anxiety disorder anxiety management skills such as relaxation techniques and positive self-talk and imagery. We combine this with gradual graded exposure to the feared situation and prevention of the avoidance response, a key ingredient in the treatment of these disorders. For posttraumatic stress disorder clients a working through of the traumatic memories in a safe, supportive setting is often helpful. These settings can include support groups, outpatient therapy, groups, or, in extreme situations, inpatient settings. Aerobic exercise often is beneficial, as is appropriate nutrition emphasizing serotonin-enhancing foods. The provider will also need to assess the family and intervene where needed. Unusual rituals or refusing to leave the home strains even the best of families. We are also impressed by the high rates of codependency and other marital difficulties in this population and feel strongly that these issues need to be assessed and treated as necessary. Codependents trying to "manage the unmanageable," including an addicted family member, will be anxious. In fact, our experience suggests that some anxiety disorders, especially if vague in presentation, are "really" severe examples of codependency.

We use a kind, gentle, but firm approach to nudge clients with an anxiety disorder one step at a time, one day at a time. Directing these clients to focus and repeating material with checks for comprehension help deal with concentration difficulties. Unless severe, most people can best be treated on an outpatient basis.

The exception to the "no medication" rule is for panic attacks. Panic attacks often respond well to treatment with antidepressants, especially when combined with the therapy measures described above (7,8). Luckily, the antidepressants, especially the nonsedating ones, appear to have little abuse potential. Buspar®, a new antianxiety agent reportedly with no abuse potential, is now available (9), but we would prefer additional data before recommending such a medication.

We have found that chemical dependency counseling with this population requires a particularly well-coordinated team approach. Psychiatric interventions need to emphasize the need for abstinence. Chemical dependency counselors need to recognize the special issues associated with agoraphobia and the panic disorders. Attendance at A.A. meetings should include an understanding of the acute fear of large groups of people that these clients experience. Small intimate A.A. meetings are helpful. A counselor, sponsor, or supportive family member may want to accompany the person to his first few meetings. Step work needs to emphasize the synergistic quality of substance abuse. The use of minor tranquilizers such as Valium® or Xanax® can actually exacerbate the anxiety disorder with prolonged use and interfere with behavior therapy (8).

We generally use standard step work with anxiety-disordered persons. The concept of powerlessness in Step 1 needs to emphasize the paradox of this step. By accepting that they are not in control of their drug or alcohol abuse and by accepting that their attempts are to control the uncontrollable, these individuals can begin to make progress. The first three steps of Alcoholics Anonymous can assist the client in letting go of strong control issues and in developing a calmer "what will be will be" attitude accompanied by a sense of faith that occurs in Step 2. This faith can help the person suffering from an anxiety disorder to begin to believe that "things eventually go the way they are supposed to" and that "all my worrying does is upset me, it doesn't change people, places or things." Working the Twelve Steps assists in developing personal responsibility for recovery. One way of demonstrating responsibility is for clients to notify their physician of their addiction and to inform them of their need for total abstinence from mood altering chemicals.

Many clients suffering from posttraumatic stress disorder benefit from Steps 4 and 5, since these steps allow them to relive and then let go. However, the counselor should go slowly with clients with a history of severe trauma, especially if it occurred at a young age (see borderlines, Chapter 6). Some of these persons experience strong emotion and need to take a slow pace.

In our experience, persons with anxiety disorders, especially the more severe ones, are at high risk for relapse. Many experience residual anxiety symptoms and are tempted to seek relief by renewed use of chemicals or the use of other compulsive behaviors such as gambling or overeating. Working an ongoing program is a key to success for these persons.

THE CLIENT WITH AN ORGANIC MENTAL DISORDER

The essential feature of an organic mental disorder is a psychological or behavioral abnormality associated with transient or permanent dysfunction of the brain and judged to be caused by a specific organic factor.

The term organic mental disorder encompasses an enormous variety of symptoms and causes. Symptoms can be relatively global as in a dementia, where many different cognitive and behavioral difficulties exist. Other disorders evidence more specific symptoms, such as organic hallucinosis with its vivid and persistent hallucinations. The course can be acute as with a delirium caused by an acute infection or by intoxication (a kind of delirium) caused by recent use of psychoactive or other chemicals. The course can also be chronic as with a dementia from head injury or such diseases as Alzheimer's. Finally, the presenting symptoms can include obvious cognitive problems such as difficulty remembering recent events and inability to care for self, to more subtle disturbances of mood and behavior. We limit our discussion to more chronic organic mental disorders resulting from chemical use and to the mild to moderate dementias whatever the cause. Delirium, acute withdrawal, severe intoxification, and severe dementia require medical and nursing management to insure safety and health. Care providers will more likely need to deal with dually diagnosed persons experiencing the less transient disorders associated with prolonged chemical use or other etiological factors.

Some chemically abusing or dependent individuals can evidence a prolonged withdrawal syndrome (10). Anxiety, depression, cognitive difficulties, physiologic symptoms, irritability, emotional lability, and transient or chronic psychotic symptoms can characterize this syndrome. Withdrawal from alcohol and, most especially, the sedatives such as the benzodiazepines can produce such states. Clinicians have reported benzodiazepine withdrawal psychoses as late as 14 days after the beginning of abstinence. Cessation of stimulant or hallucinogenic drugs often causes a prolonged withdrawal syndrome characterized by serious depression as well as irritability and anxiety. This appears to be especially true of cocaine and crack users. The existence of a prolonged withdrawal syndrome associated with marijuana is controversial but our clinical experience has convinced us that chronic pot smokers experience such difficulties.

Generally standard chemical dependency programs and staff have experience dealing with clients experiencing these effects. Adequate nutrition, reassurance and support, and physical interventions such as mild exercise or hot tubs are helpful. These staff also know, intuitively and explicitly, that such individuals will show mild difficulties absorbing, processing, and using new information and experience, and they adjust their expectations and inputs appropriately.

Occasionally, the client will show a severe prolonged withdrawal syndrome marked by psychosis or assaultive or suicidal behavior and will require the higher levels of care and the diagnostic possibilities that dual diagnosis program can offer. One phenomenon of particular interest is a long-lasting, schizophrenic-like condition that persists after prolonged heavy stimulant or hallucinogen use. Characterized by psychotic symptoms but with social approach behavior intact, some investigators have suggested that the phenomenon of "kindling" might account for this particular condition and others (see Ref. 11). These chemicals appear to produce their effects in the same brain tracts that are associated with schizophrenia. Chronic stimulant or hallucinogen use appears to produce permanently damaged, easily stimulated neurons in these tracts that produce this schizophrenic-like condition, according to this model. Other investigators have found evidence of a possible genetic predisposition in the chronic psychosis associated with drug abuse (12).

Whatever the cause, this condition can last months or years and requires interventions similar to those used with schizophrenia. However, in our experience these individuals are more amenable to treatment than many persons with schizophrenia because they bring personal strengths and skills to the treatment (including ease in relating to other people) not always found in those suffering from schizophrenia. They also tend to have a profound appreciation of the losses caused by their chemical use, which makes "denial-busting" somewhat easier.

Dementia is the prototypical organic mental disorder that raises issues of the need for dual diagnosis treatment. The essential features of dementia are memory difficulties and other cognitive impairments as well as profound personality deterioration. Table 7 presents the signs and symptoms of dementia in more detail.

Chronic alcoholism leads to a progressive deterioration of cognitive abilities. This deterioration occurs surprisingly early (as soon as 30 years of age) and seems related more to amounts consumed in one setting than to the frequency and duration of alcohol use. Alcoholism produces impaired nonverbal abstract thinking and visual–motor slowing as well as short- and long-term memory problems. Auditory--verbal abilities are relatively intact but where these sorts of tasks require new learning chronic alcoholics show difficulties in these areas as well. Some research evidence exists for similar impairments among chronic users of other sedative hypnotics. Interestingly, the research evidence does not indicate significant lasting cognitive impairments with chronic use of marijuana, opiates, stimulants, and hallucinogens. The limited research on inhalant users has also found evidence for cognitive damage as a group (13).

We have frequently seen dementia caused by head trauma among the dual diagnosis clients suffering from an organic mental disorder. Some chemically dependent individuals either grew up in or are currently in family situations where physical abuse has been so severe that brain damage has resulted. We treated one "slow" individual with a history of repeated beatings by an abusive husband. Her husband would sit on the client and smash her head repeatedly into the floor. A "B" student in high school, these beatings and her intense alcohol abuse produced a moderate dementia. In addition, intoxicated individuals often have a history of repeated head injury in falls, fights, and other accidents. Antisocial personalities, with their penchant for excitement, are also individuals who often have head injuries after an escapade such as a bar fight or motorcycle race gone sour. This plus their strong tendency to be chemically involved makes for an interesting and challenging "triple" diagnosis client.

We should mention a common disorder associated with cognitive deficits first evident in infancy, childhood, or adolescence because of its association with chemical abuse. Children with attention-deficit with or without hyperactivity disorder (ADD-H; ADD) show inappropriate inattention, impulsiveness, and rates of motor behavior that interfere with their ability to tolerate situations requiring controlled behavior for successful academic or interpersonal outcomes. In addition to their cognitive failures, which often result in depression, acting-out behavior, and membership in socially deviant groups, many of these persons will continue to show symptoms of attention deficit disorder and hyperactivity into adulthood and not outgrow the syndrome as formerly thought (4). These individuals, in our experience,

TABLE 7
Dementia

Feeling	Thinking	Behavior	Interpersonal relations and role functioning	Chemical use
Sometimes anxiety or depression	Short- and long-term memory impairment	Often poor impulse control with actions that are potentially harmful	Often increased conflict with significant others	Polysubstance abuse but generally the more accessible chemicals such as alcohol or marijuana
Sometimes apathy or indifference	Impaired abstract thinking and judgment	Often outbursts, tantrums, assaults	Impairment in work and social activities, poor coping with stressors	Increased use of stimulants in ADD clients
Sometimes emotional lability and irritability	Impaired auditory–verbal and/or visual–motor abilities	Sometimes disorganized or perseverative behavior	In serious cases, impaired activities of daily living	
	Sometimes paranoid thinking	Change or exaggeration in personality style		
	Slower information processing			

appear to be at high risk for substance abuse. More than once spouses and providers have approached us in our workshops about the treatment of an adult with a history of this disorder who was also chemically involved.

The variety of organic mental disorders requires careful, upfront assessment to determine the best treatment approach. A person with severe cognitive impairment who requires continual and constant supervision makes the issue of dual diagnosis treatment irrelevant. The caretaker (preferably one without a chemical use problem) can insure abstinence by stopping access. Moderate impairment where the individual requires some supervision almost always requires dual diagnosis treatment. Mild impairment (where judgment remains relatively intact, where the capacity for independent living remains, and the performance of self-care activities is adequate, but where there are work and social difficulties) requires evaluation regarding impulse control and ability to learn at reasonable rates and with standard procedures to determine the need for dual diagnosis treatment. Serious learning difficulties and/or poor impulse control suggest the need for specialized treatment.

Other considerations for treatment planning are the history and course of the disorder. Especially for younger persons, recovery from traumatic head injuries can be substantial. Abstinence from alcohol often results in at least the partial return of cognitive abilities. On the other hand, a rapidly progressive dementia such as early-onset Alzheimer's makes investment of time, energy, and resources in chemical dependency treatment questionable. A good rule of thumb is to determine the rate of improvement or deterioration over a 6-month period and to expect little additional improvement after 1 year (13). Abstinence is essential for any improvement to occur.

Consequently, we like to inquire about the following to determine the need for specialized dual diagnosis treatment: diagnosis of the organic mental disorder, if known; ability to provide self-care; capacity for independent living; impulse control problems such as tantrums and assaultiveness; ability to take direction; response to new situations and material; change in mental status over at least 6 months, if applicable; response to previous rehabilitation efforts; level of functioning prior to the onset of the organic mental disorder; and the availability of supervised living situations. We combine these data to make a determination of a client's treatment needs and potential for successful treatment.

Psychological testing can be of invaluable assistance in assessing general level of cognitive functioning as well as pinpointing specific deficits and capabilities. We tailor our material to make use of any strengths that the client has in visual–motor or auditory–verbal modalities. Personality testing can also pinpoint emotional issues likely to interfere with treatment such as hopelessness, passivity, or disinhibition.

We generally recommend the use of medications with the organic mental disorders only when there are strong clinical indications. Medication, especially at high levels, can increase confusion and agitation. Antipsychotic medications can be useful with psychotic symptoms or emotional lability. A seizure disorder requires antiseizure medication. We do try to determine whether the seizures were secondary to alcohol or other sedative withdrawal and not correctly diagnosed at the time. We have also seen a few individuals abuse the seizure medication Phenobarbitol (especially where they have abused alcohol or the benzodiazepines and then experience difficulty obtaining these preferred chemicals). Use of seizure medications with the potential dual diagnosis client requires careful evaluation and monitoring.

The use of stimulant medication such as Ritalin® or Cylert® (the generally accepted treatment for this disorder) for the dually diagnosed client with an attention-deficit disorder remains controversial. Reports in the literature claim successful use of this medication to control ADD symptoms in adult clients with a history of chemical abuse and dependency but without relapse or abuse of the prescribed medicine (14). In our experience, a minority of attention-deficit disorders do respond to treatment with lithium or the antidepressants. (Are these persons really atypical affective disorders?) We generally prefer to use behavioral interventions with ADD clients except in very severe cases where these interventions have failed. We combine this with extensive client counseling regarding the risks to their sobriety of using this medication. This is an area needing more research.

We use many of the same general interventions for these clients that we would use for the person suffering from schizophrenia. Prompts and praise from staff are useful, as are the use of cuing devices such as checklists, reminder cards, and daily schedules. Keeping material simple and concrete, repeating material frequently, and applying new material and practicing new behavior on a situation-by-situation basis is also useful. Watch out for the "talks-good-but-can't-apply-it" syndrome. Some clients with subtle dementias still have intact verbal skills but cannot generalize concepts or have learned to "fake good" in superficial interactions. Test them for comprehension and performance. Relaxation training and cuing strategies are useful for ADD clients. We use audiotapes for those with reading and writing difficulties and movies and role playing for those with auditory–verbal problems. Appendix 1 presents specialized step work for these people.

We supplement this treatment with skills training and educational/ vocational assistance where needed. We also do grief work around the client's losses and build damaged egos with identification of strengths and provision of opportunities for success.

Abstinence is the only goal for the person with an organic mental disorder. A brain especially vulnerable to the toxic effects of chemicals and compromised in its abilities does not need more of the same.

We have found a variety of substance abuse patterns in this population. In our experience, alcohol is often the drug of choice with demented clients. Clients diagnosed ADD often present addicted to stimulants (15).

Step work needs to be concrete and simple. We use flash cards and simple one-line questions and answers with this group. Generally the step work we use with the schizophrenic individual is most useful with this group (see Appendix 1). These people can participate fully in Alcoholics Anonymous meetings. They may need a support person to accompany them to meetings and assure that they arrive in the right location. The support person can also help prevent rambling and incoherent comments during the meeting. Nonverbal as well as verbal cuing on the part of the counselor can condition the client to develop good group behavior.

Prognosis for this group depends on the particular disorder and its severity. Moderately impaired alcoholics are at high risk for treatment failure according to the research studies (13). This probably reflects both the progression of the disease and the failure of treatment approaches that rely on some cognitive capability. Very labile, assaultive individuals are also difficult to manage, with the focus becoming their behavior and with the disruption to the program being too much to tolerate. On the other hand, we have had gratifying successes where we have carefully tailored our approach to the specific individual and provided intensive, structured aftercare arrangements. It is above all important to remember not to fall into the trap of whether or not the organic patient is "truly" alcoholic. Any use of alcohol or drugs in this population will only add to deterioration of what functional thinking they possess. Therefore, the counselor should view any use as problematic and a dual diagnosis approach, with abstinence as the goal, is necessary.

REFERENCES

1. Schneier, F. R., and Siris, S. G. Review of psychoactive substance use and abuse in schizophrenia. *Journal of Nervous and Mental Disease, 175* (11), 641–652, 1987.

2. Estroff, T. W., Dackis, C. A., Gold, M. S., et al. Drug abuse and bipolar disorder. *International Journal of Psychiatric Medicine, 15*, 37–40, 1985.
3. Liepman, M. R., Nirenberg, T. D., Porges, R. E., and Wartenberg, A.A. Depression associated with substance abuse. In O. G. Cameron (Ed.), *Presentations of Depression.* Wiley, New York, 1987.
4. American Psychiatric Association. *Diagnostic and Statistical Manual of Mental Disorders,* third edition, revised. American Psychiatric Association, Washington, D.C., 1987.
5. Hesselbrock, M. N., Meyer, R. E., and Keener, J. J. Psychopathology in hospitalized alcoholics. *Archives of General Psychiatry, 42,* 1050–1055, 1985.
6. Gianni, A. J., Malone, D. A., Gianni, M. C. et al. Treatment of depression in chronic cocaine and phencyclidine abuse with desipramine. *Journal of Clinical Pharmacology, 26,* 211–214, 1986.
7. Quitkin, F. M., and Rabbin, J. G. Hidden psychiatric diagnoses in the alcoholic. In J. Soloman (Ed.), *Alcoholism and Clinical Psychiatry.* Plenum Press, New York, pp. 129–139, 1982.
8. Kranzler, H. R., and Liebowitz, N. R. Anxiety and depression in substance abuse. *Medical Clinics of North America, 72(4),* 867–885, 1988.
9. Meyer, R. E. Anxiolytics and the alcoholic patient. *Journal of Studies of Alcoholism, 47,* 269–273, 1986.
10. Peyser, H. S. Alcoholism and clinical psychiatry. In S. E. Gitlow and H. S. Peyser (Eds.), *Alcoholism: A Practical Treatment Guide.* Grune & Stratton, Philadelphia, 1988.
11. Dilsauer, S. The pathophysiologies of substance abuse and affective disorders: An integrative model. *Journal of Clinical Psychopharmacology, 7,* 1–10, 1987.
12. Tsuang, T. S., Simpson, J. C., and Kronfol, Z. Subtypes of drug abuse with psychosis. *Archives of General Psychiatry, 39,* 141–147, 1982.
13. Grant, I., and Reed, R. Neuropsychology of alcohol and drug abuse. In A. Alterman (Ed.), *Substance Abuse and Psychopathology.* Plenum Press, New York, 1985.
14. Wender, P. H., Reimherr, F. W. and Wood, D. R. Attention deficit disorder ("minimal brain dysfunction") in adults. *Archives of General Psychiatry, 38,* 449–456, 1981.
15. Extein, I. L., Dackis, C. A., Gold, M. S., and Pottash, A. L. C. Depression in drug addicts and alcoholics. In I. L. Extein and M. S. Gold (Eds.), *Medical Mimics of Psychiatric Disorders.* American Psychiatric Press, Washington, D.C., 1986.

6

<hr style="width:20%">

Selected Personality Disorders

The purpose of this chapter is to discuss dual diagnosis treatment of clients who are chemically dependent and have certain kinds of coexisting personality disorders. The chapter focuses on passive–aggressive, antisocial, and borderline personality disorders. These disorders frequently coexist with chemical dependency and they are ones that present the greatest challenge to service providers because individuals with these disorders use "acting out" defenses.

THE ACTING OUT PERSONALITY DISORDERS

Personality is defined as enduring patterns of perceiving, relating to, and thinking about oneself and the world that manifest themselves in a wide range of important situations. Everyone has acted in a passive–aggressive, antisocial, or even borderline manner at one time or another. A personality pattern becomes "disordered" only when the pattern is inflexible and maladaptive, leads to substantial subjective distress or functional impairment, and characterizes the person's long-term functioning in a variety of situations (1).

The term "acting out" refers to behavioral patterns that have an angry, hostile tone, that violate social conventions regarding appropriate ways to relate to others, and that result in negative consequences to self and others. These behaviors range in severity from subtle insults to tantrums to physical abuse of self or others. The negative consequences include such things as rejection or retaliation by others, legal charges, or the risk of injury to self or others. Persons who show these patterns also deny that they have a problem and use thinking errors to justify their behavior. This makes them difficult to treat.

The passive–aggressive, antisocial, and borderline personality disorders exhibit this overall pattern and share a number of common characteristics. Anger is a key affect for these individuals and tends to characterize many of their important interactions. All these individuals also tend to report chronic feelings of unhappiness and alienation from others as well as conflicts with authority and family discord, both past and present. Most of these individuals have major control issues, being prone to perceive others as trying to control them and being highly invested in controlling others. They also evidence strong patterns of denial. These individuals are also at high risk for developing chemical dependency. When you add the denial and control issues normally associated with chemical dependency to those same characteristics found in the personality disordered client, you have double denial.

Chemically abusing or dependent individuals also develop acting out behavior patterns as their disease progresses and this appears especially true for drug abusers as compared to alcoholics (2–4). For example, the thinking errors discussed in Chapter 3 are characteristic of both chemically dependent individuals and individuals with one of the acting out personality disorders. Consequently, establishing the diagnosis of a personality disorder in a chemically dependent client must take into account the issues discussed in Chapter 4. For example, individuals with only a chemical use or dependency disorder show improvement with abstinence while, the client with an acting out personality disorder shows difficulties prior to substance abuse and shows a substantial intensification of all acting out behaviors and defenses when using (see Ref. 5).

Dysfunctional behavior caused by a brain disease such as schizophrenia has a certain logic that allows providers to think in kinder terms about these mentally ill clients. Personality disorders often strike providers as being different. Why do these individuals act in maladaptive ways? From an objective point of view these ways of relating seem maladaptive. These clients often tempt the provider to attribute malign motives to these clients since such behaviors seem deliberate, willful and/or controllable. Such attributions can lead providers to blame their clients, become frustrated, and lose their objectivity.

We set great stock in understanding the subjective world view of the personality-disordered client. This approach helps us select treatment interventions and remain objective. We find it useful to employ different kinds of circles to represent the person's sense of self and the world. The solidity and overlap of the circles represent the person's sense of boundaries. The size of the circles captures the person's relative sense of power and control of the self versus the world. For example, we would represent the fearful person suffering from psychotic disorder such as schizophrenia like this:

Self   World

People with a psychotic disorder have a poor concept of boundaries and difficulty sorting out self and world. They also experience the world as large and overwhelming. Treatment needs to help these individuals firm up their boundaries, separate self and world, and increase their ability to cope. Medication, reality orientation, structure, and skills building all help achieve these objectives.

So far in our discussion, we have emphasized the general similarities of the passive–aggressive, antisocial, and borderline personalities. The rest of the chapter discusses their differences and the differences in dual diagnosis treatment these disorders require. We make use of circle diagrams to help clarify and explain the written material that we have provided. Table 8 also provides information on the differences among these three disorders.

THE CLIENT WITH A PASSIVE–AGGRESSIVE PERSONALITY DISORDER

The central feature of the passive–aggressive personality disorder is passive resistance to required social and occupational performance (1). Passive–aggressive individuals typically lack confidence in their ability to meet their own needs and are dependent on others to provide psychological support. These individuals also feel that direct requests and straightforward negotiation of issues when conflict arises will lead to rejection and distancing by others. Often passive–aggressive persons will go above and beyond the call of duty and perform all kinds of caretaking-of-other activities in an indirect attempt to coerce love and gain acceptance. When others do not respond the "right" way (and they often do not), the passive–aggressive person becomes chronically irritable and can adopt a martyr attitude. Caught between his/her need to "belong" to someone who will meet his/her needs and the belief that

TABLE 8
Characteristics of Passive–Aggressive, Antisocial, and Borderline Personality Disorders

Area	Passive–Aggressive	Antisocial	Borderline
Affect	Overcontrolled hostility	Angry intimidation	Angry self-harm
Worldview	"I do everything right and they still act this way"	"If you don't do what I want, you'll be sorry"	"I've got to get you before you get me"
	"I don't deserve this"	"I deserve it all"	"I don't deserve to exist"
	"I'm fine, ignore the tears"	"They're the ones with the problem"	"Help me, help me, but you can't"
Presenting problem	Depression, somatization sedative dependence, codependency	Legal difficulties, polysubstance abuse and dependence, parasitic relationships	Self-harm, weird thinking and behavior, episodic poly-substance abuse, hot/cold relationships
Social functioning	Consistent underachievement	Episodic achievement	Gross dysfunctioning
Motivation	Belonging	Self-esteem	Safety
Defenses	Repression	Rationalization, projection	Autistic fantasy

assertive expression of feelings will result in isolation, the anger of the passive–aggressive leaks out in a thousand different ways. These are the people who forget their counseling appointment, arrive late, or somehow just could not get their homework done. At the same time, they excuse their noncompliance by blaming external events or other people.

The passive–aggressive often presents with feelings of anxiety and depression as well as with vague somatic complaints. The failure to obtain what they need in a consistent and direct fashion results in these negative feelings. Complaints of headaches, backaches, and other so-called functional (no medical basis) body symptoms represent an indirect way of getting attention and concern. These complaints also represent the result of "stuffing" angry feelings and the resultant chronic stress. Many passive–aggressive individuals will also present with marital and family difficulties. Codependency is a common issue for these clients (this is not to say that all codependents have passive–aggressive personality disorder). They can be in relationships where the significant other is abusing chemicals or abusing the client, yet the passive–aggressive person will stay in the relationship, perhaps nagging the substance abuser or burning the toast, but behaviorally enabling the behavior and picking up after the significant other.

Using our circles metaphor, a passive–aggressive person looks like this:

Self   World

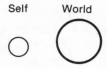

These clients are in touch with reality and have ego strength, firm boundaries, and a clear sense of the separation between self and world. However, they feel small and powerless in their relationship to the world.

These clients typically have experienced a family environment where others valued them only when they did the "right" things, and the right things did not include the direct expression of feelings and needs and discussion of problems. Family members typically met assertion with subtle discounting, withdrawal of attention and affection, and criticism of the person (see Ref. 6).

The general goal of therapy with these clients is to build up their sense of self in relationship to the world. The "three A's" summarize the strategies that we have found useful. First, *ally* these clients with others who will meet their dependency needs. Therapists who encourage divorce or separation in the first session with a client in a codependent relationship will trigger passive resistance. These clients need the supportive alliances that can stem from the therapeutic relationship, attendance at support groups, or the establishment of a friendship network. Second, make them *aware* of how their indirect ways of relating are not working. Gently calling these clients on their failure to follow through on homework assignments, reviewing their relationships with others, and encouraging the reading of books about codependency and assertiveness are useful in accomplishing this. Finally, *assertion* work can help these clients understand that they have rights and develop direct ways of relating to others. Challenging them to deal directly with the provocative behavior of others is useful.

In our experience, passive–aggressive persons are at risk for developing chemical dependency, with a preference for alcohol and sedative/hypnotics. Many come from alcoholic families. In addition, the state induced by alcohol and the sedative hypnotics resembles the defense of repression commonly used by passive–aggressive people. That "what bad feelings?/I'll deal with it tomorrow" defense strategy is analogous to the blanking-out function served by this class of chemicals. Finally, a passive–aggressive person's presentation emphasizes being "nice." Nice people drink at the country club or take medications their doctor prescribed. Nice people don't buy heroin from a pusher.

A Twelve Step program is highly effective for these individuals. You need not modify step work in any particular way. Dealing with issues of covert control via step work is very therapeutic. The recovery model also provides excellent social support and practice in the direct expression of feelings. Combined with assertion work, the package is powerful and effective (7). Just be careful to be clear and explicit in your expectations and hold clients accountable for completing assignments. Be careful to talk about cross-addiction issues (as between alcohol and Valium®). Also talk about the fact that prescription medications are drugs with potential for abuse and about the need for clients to take responsibility for informing physicians about their addiction. Family education and attendance at Al-Anon or Alateen reinforces the individual work with the client. Watch out for a "codependent run" in which other family members and the client join together to convince themselves they cannot survive without the client out of treatment and back home. Frequent, brief family conferences are helpful here.

Standard chemical dependency programs can successfully treat most passive–aggressive people. Only when there is a suicidal crisis or a risk of harm from an abusive spouse will dual diagnosis issues or settings be necessary. We remember admitting one suicidal woman who needed the locked doors of our inpatient unit to keep out an abusive husband with a reputation for beating her up as well as assaulting treatment personnel. Needless to say, one focus of treatment was the need of the client to set limits on this spouse by obtaining a restraining order and considering a divorce.

THE CLIENT WITH AN ANTISOCIAL PERSONALITY DISORDER

A pattern of irresponsible behavior and behavior that consistently violates rights of others, social norms, and laws is the cardinal feature of the antisocial personality disorder (1). These individuals have an extremely inflated sense of their own worth and prerogatives, with little capacity for a genuine empathetic relationship with other persons. The antisocial personality feels little guilt over the trail of wreckage left in his/her wake. Such individuals feel they are never responsible because it's always "someone else's fault" or there was a "good reason why I did that." Maintenance of their inflated sense of self is a prime motivation of the antisocial personality. Looking good, being cool, and being better that anyone else is a preoccupation of the antisocial personality. Their "image" is central to their psychological workings. Thrill and excitement seeking are other key motivators. Boredom is the enemy of the person with an antisocial personality disorder. Finally, to antisocial individuals "life is a game" and the object is to win, preferably in the most exciting, grandiose style possible. Even more importantly, they want others to lose and for the loser to acknowledge this.

Antisocial clients sometimes get depressed, even to the point of being suicidal, and many have a history of suicide attempts (2). This depression is typically in response to getting caught by the police or otherwise suffering the negative consequences of their behavior. This depression is also brief and will pass as the individual with an antisocial personality disorder regroups and redefines the problem as everyone else's. Needless to say, legal difficulties are common, as are marital and family difficulties. Generally it's a significant other with the complaints. Antisocial personalities are just fine with a relationship as long as the other person meets their needs and does not dare presume to want anything in return.

The self/world relationship of the antisocial looks like this:

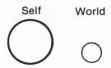

Self   World

Boundaries are firm, perhaps too firm, and the antisocial is very clear on the difference between self and world. Simultaneously such individuals believe they are more important and powerful than anyone else and they intend to stay that way.

Where do antisocials come from? Sometimes they seem to come out of the blue, with good childhood experiences and from a fine family. Recent studies have indicated that a history of neglect is important in many cases (8). One can imagine neglected children deciding that they come first ("since no one else cares") and that rules do not matter ("since they have not given me any reason to follow any rules"). Other authorities suggest that there might be a genetic component to the thrill-seeking aspect of this personality type, an aspect that fuels their behavior (4). However, by the time they hit the provider's office, etiology is of little concern. Discussion of the "why" serves only to provide the antisocial personality with excuses for his/her behavior and takes the focus off *the individual's* need to be responsible.

The goal of therapy with the antisocial personality is *not* to create an empathetic, self-sacrificing individual with guilt. You will never achieve this. The goal is to adapt the sociopathy so that antisocial clients come to believe that playing by the rules of society can actually make them look better in the long run, giving them greater success and helping them stay out of trouble. An emphasis on honesty is the first priority. The challenge for the provider is to convince antisocials that it is in their best interest to change, as they are making too many mistakes. In a sense the provider must chip away at the antisocial's self and make the world bigger.

The "three C's" summarize the treatment strategies to use for working with the antisocial personality (see Ref. 9). You must first *corral* them. Without the "walls" provided by locked doors and/or legal mandates, most antisocials will generally not stick around for treatment. Don't get fooled by the "I-got-caught" moment of remorse. This seldom lasts but can be most helpful to provide a moment of truth. Age can be important here. Intervention in childhood and early adolescence is often effective because the lifestyle is less entrenched and authority figures retain more control. Other antisocials experience a prolonged depressive crisis in their late 30s or their early 40s as their physiology slows down and their long-term failure to maintain themselves as "king of the mountain" sinks in. Even in these cases, someone else with something the antisocial personality wants is most often forcing treatment.

Confront the antisocial personality. The provider needs to chip away at his defenses, helping him face how he thinks about the world and how this really has not gotten him what he wants. Remember, such cases want tangible rewards, not world peace. The thinking errors presented in Chapter 3 will give you a useful framework for confronting the process of their thinking and for avoiding power struggles around content. Don't argue the number of legal convictions. Instead, point out the lying by commission, omission, or assent. Do this repeatedly but with a gentle, supportive tone. Position yourself in relation to your client as helpful and not as a critical authority figure. We have found it most helpful to begin the session by developing a positive rapport. Discuss with the client what *his/her* goals of counseling are, that is, "staying out of jail," "getting my wife off my back," and so forth.

Once you have found a mutual goal, discuss how you might be helpful in assisting him/her to reach this goal. Establish that the two of you will be working together to achieve the goal by examining thinking patterns of the client that are at the core of the problem. Obtain agreement from the client that he/she wants you to point out mistakes in thinking, or thinking errors that get in the way of achieving his/her goal. Then, when the client is displaying a thinking error such as blaming, minimizing, rationalizing, or lying, point it out without engaging in a power struggle. If the person resists, restate the treatment contract. If working in a group with these clients, establish the group norm of pointing out each others' thinking errors as helpful peer confrontation. This can be extremely powerful.

Finally, provide *consequences* for this behavior. These consequences need to be immediate, concrete, and to make use of the antisocial's need to look good and feel excited. These individuals do not easily tolerate a delay of gratification. They do not care about what you think unless you can back this up with something real. They are also slow learners and require repetition of consequences to convince them that it is their behavior that is causing the problem. Use access to activities, visiting privileges, jobs, and other immediate concrete awards. Group contingencies (all lose privileges if a member fails to exhibit certain behavior) are useful in enlisting other antisocial clients to apply strong peer pressure for prosocial behavior.

Antisocial personalities are at extremely high risk for chemical dependency (4,10). They often use any and all substances and are common in a variety of service settings. Apart from the stimulation provided by the chemicals themselves, a lifestyle with the ups and downs of heavy chemical involvement and the money, violence, and criminal status of illegal drug trafficking can be very attractive to the excitement-driven antisocial. Many young antisocials, suspended from school, in conflict with the family, and bored by the thought of working at a fast-food restaurant, associate with marginal groups where drug use is the norm. In turn, chemical use adds gasoline to the fire, reinforcing their distorted, self-centered world view.

During the assessment process assume that very little of the data being provided by the antisocial client are accurate. Check out everything with collateral contacts and use urine drug screens and other objective tools. Remember, the telephone can be your friend with these clients. Continued vigilance of this sort must also be maintained throughout treatment and aftercare.

The Twelve Step recovery model can be very effective with these individuals when combined with the strategies outlined above. Step 1 is crucial and gets at a core treatment issue. We insist on *surrender* by the client. Clients need to understand that they are not in control of either chemical use or the consequences administered to them. It is important that the antisocial clients learn to identify exactly how their drinking/using behavior was out of control, how they had lost control over their behavior when drinking and using, and how they are powerless. Requiring explicit examples is helpful. We also require clients to identify the thinking errors they use to justify their chemical use and other antisocial behavior. "How do you blame, manipulate, lie, etc., to justify your use and control others, and what are the negative consequences for you of that behavior?" is the key treatment focus. We proceed with further step work, always with an eye toward the manifestation of thinking errors. Examples of specialized step work for Steps 1–4 can be found in Appendix 1. Sometimes you can also convince the antisocial person to be the very *best* recovering person in the world, chairing great A.A. meetings and giving talks to civic groups.

Outpatient work with the antisocial personality can be difficult. Outpatient providers seldom have the external controls necessary to enforce compliance. Standard chemical dependency programs usually manage the thinking errors of the chemically dependent individual well, but, in our experience, the genuine antisocial personality is too disruptive for most chemical dependency programs to treat success-fully. Programs with expertise in dealing with antisocials (and the ability to restrain acting out) and with the backup provided by parental consent or court mandates are generally necessary for success in the early stages of treatment and until acute denial issues have been worked through.

Remember, antisocials get clean and sober for their own reasons, not your reasons. Go for prorecovery behavior, and do not worry about motivation. It is highly unlikely that antisocials will develop genuine remorse and altruistic reasons for staying clean and sober. However, they may be interested if it will help them win at poker, make more money, or stay out of jail.

THE CLIENT WITH A BORDERLINE
PERSONALITY DISORDER

Borderline personality disorders represent one of the greatest chal-lenges to the treatment provider. These individuals are "stably unsta-ble," with wide-ranging and persistent instability of self-image, inter-personal relationships, and mood (1). At the core level the borderline client is a deprived, damaged, fragile child who was typically trauma-tized by a very dysfunctional family situation. Ambivalence is the essence of borderline person's existence. These people desperately seek the love and nurturing they never received as a child. Yet, while reaching out, they also fear they will be abused and abandoned. Those suffering from a borderline personality disorder organize themselves around safety issues, trying to balance getting their needs met with a fear of these significant others by using various safety operations. These safety operations very often take the form of antisocial defenses, which attempt to combine entanglement with others with the safety provided by manipulation and acting out (11). The counselor attempting therapeutic closeness and rapport may experience a very intense negative response by the client. Pulling back elicits another intense response from the borderline individual. The on-again, off-again quality of therapy can be very frustrating for the counselor. "Help me, help me, but you can't" is the common message of the borderline client.

The borderline person is crisis-prone and polysymptomatic. Self-harm behavior, unusual thinking with a psychotic-like flavor, eating disorders, and somatic complaints are some of the more common problems. Also common are involvement in abusive relationships and in relationships with a hot/cold quality. Quite often the end of such a relationship triggers the crisis. Borderlines are typically heavy users of human services but often with little long-term benefit.

The world view of the borderline client looks like this:

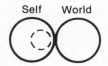

Self   World

The borderline client combines characteristics of the antisocial, neurotic, and psychotic conditions. Antisocial defenses maintain the illusion of firm boundaries and power in the face of an unsafe world. The borderline is quite often angry, manipulative, self-centered, and shows various thinking errors. But underneath this puffed-up veneer is a scared self that feels not only small and powerless but also vulnerable to being engulfed by the world. As counselors, we sense the desperate, needy, and terrified part within this person but get entangled in his/her defenses.

Both theoretical speculations and an increasing amount of research indicate that a severely dysfunctional family provokes the borderline condition. Typically people with borderline personalities have experienced not only emotional neglect but also intense and prolonged physical and sexual abuse (8,12,13). One way to conceptualize borderline personalities is to consider them a profound and chronic kind of posttraumatic stress disorder (14). In a sense, persons with borderline personalities grew up in a war zone.

Within this framework, the goal of treatment is to help a victim become a *survivor*. Heavy confrontation of their antisocial defenses and prompting them to recall the trauma only revictimize these individuals and are *not* the way to proceed. We use the "three S's" to guide our therapeutic strategies with borderline clients.

The first objective is to provide *safety* for the person. In times of crisis this often means inpatient treatment. We have a preference for relatively short-stays to avoid regression and further dependence. Kind but firm limits with the frame of *safety* are necessary and useful for these clients who are out of control and view limit-setting as punishment and engulfment. We use anti-harm contracts extensively, sometimes contracting hour by hour in inpatient settings and week by week in outpatient settings. We help the individual identify and use sources of social support such as a case manager, the crisis line, and issues groups such as A.A. and survivor-of-incest groups. We also help them pinpoint situations or events likely to trigger a self-destructive crisis and plan and practice alternative behaviors. A matter-of-fact message of "we will help you remain safe" is the essence of these interventions. Because borderline persons may have a crisis at any time, we attend to these issues even if the individuals are not currently in a crisis.

The second "S" stands for strengths. Many persons suffering from a borderline personality disorder never learned basic self-care skills in their family of origin. The lack of good modeling and emotional support as well as the childhood preoccupation with the trauma that they experienced produced a developmental arrest. Emphasizing accomplishment also serves to build up positive self-regard and combat the borderline's bleak self-image. We like to teach time management skills to assist borderline clients to structure their day and week. Helping them to identify and use recreational outlets and to develop and practice positive self-talk and affirmations is useful. We especially like assertiveness training, viewing this as a way to help them use words and not actions to deal with anger.

Only when the client has developed ways to maintain safety and has acquired skills do we proceed with *survivor* work (15). We start at a very intellectual level and avoid expressive, feeling-oriented approaches. We ask the person to read and attend classes about dysfunctional families and survivor issues. We run classes on issues such as secrets and brainwashing and their role in maintaining abuse. Unlike other groups of classes we give clients permission to control their exposure to these reminders of the trauma by closing the book, leaving class, or switching the topic. As this process continues, we gently and with the explicit consent of the clients question their thinking errors, especially focusing on the role of "victim" these clients often take. At all times, we take the stance that *safety* is first.

Borderline personality disordered persons are very prone to chemical dependency (4). Often coming from families where members (including the perpetrator) used chemicals extensively, sometimes given chemicals as part of the abuse scenario, and generally seeking relief from their psychic pain, those suffering a borderline personality abuse chemicals. These people often present with episodic but intense use of drugs and alcohol. The progression one sees in the classic alcoholic may be difficult to identify because of this pattern of use. Our experience when doing a substance abuse history with persons with a borderline personality is to find periods of heavy use, followed by periods of apparent abstinence when the person engaged in another compulsion centering on food, sex, gambling, or involving membership in a cult or participation in an intense "love" relationship. These people use a variety of drugs, but there is almost always some use of prescriptive medications in our experience. Physical dependence, if there is any, most likely will be on a tranquilizer, sedating antidepressant, or narcotic drug.

Abstinence must absolutely be the goal for the borderline client. We are talking a lethal combination here. Teaching the disease concept of chemical dependency not only reinforces the need for abstinence but combats their negative self-image. The notion of "sick getting well," not "bad getting good," is helpful in working with the good/bad, black/white thinking style of the borderline client.

Be careful when using autobiographies, the telling of one's "story." This process can flood these people with unmanageable feelings as they recall their trauma. In severe cases we often skip the autobiography all together. At other times we direct the person to focus only on chemical use or start at age 12 in their written history.

When utilizing the Twelve Steps we have found certain modifications helpful. When working on Step 1 we have found it important to focus more on the unmanageability of the alcohol and drug use. The counselor can assist the client to identify situations and problems that indicate that his/her chemical use was problematic and out of control. Go easy on the concept of powerlessness. Surrender terrifies these survivors. Focus *only* on powerlessness or loss of control over drugs and alcohol and avoid attempts to ask the borderline to generalize the concept of powerlessness to other areas of his/her life. This can be asked later on but only after some strengthening of alternate ways to cope and feel safe has occurred. Premature attempts to get this client to surrender will only be met with acting out and an intensification of denial.

Modifications of other steps are also useful. Step 2, "came to believe that a power greater than ourselves could restore us to sanity," is in essence a step of faith. In the alcoholic client we attempt to expand on faith and how things are looking up, now that the client is abstinent. For the borderline personality disordered person faith and a belief in a higher power are extremely difficult concepts. These persons are living life moment to moment. For them to have faith or hope that things will be any different than now is nearly impossible. What we try to do is to take this step with them in small pieces. Ask them to discuss how their drinking or using was "insane." Ask them to give three examples of positive things that have happened since not using. Ask them to find even small instances of positive events in their life since abstinence. The concept of higher power is difficult for these people and requires a great deal of individualization. Do they believe in God? Do they believe God let them down? When exploring this subject allow them the freedom to say "I feel unsafe or overwhelmed and want to stop for now."

Step 3 states that we "made a decision to turn our will and our lives over to the care of God as we understood him." We work this step with this client in the same way we would any client. We try to assist him/her in learning to try to let go of obsessional thinking and trying to overcontrol other people, places, and things. Remember to build alternate skills prior to doing this step.

We very much prefer to complete Steps 4 and 5 in a safe setting because of the regressions that can occur. Step 4 is "made a searching and fearless moral inventory of ourselves." This can be an extremely volatile step for this client. We have modified this step in the following ways: we start the inventory at age 12 and up; and we require the client to list an equal amount of positives or strengths as well as "character defects." Appendix 1 contains examples of step work for Steps 1 through 4 that are useful with the person suffering borderline personality disorder.

We encourage A.A. attendance. Persons with a borderline disorder benefit from the access to support that these meetings provide. We do predict to our clients that they might not like a particular meeting and encourage them to be in control of which meeting they attend. We discourage attendance at ACOA (Adult Children of Alcoholics) meetings until later in their recovery. The emphasis on feeling work and relative lack of structure often found at these meetings, although useful for the ACOA, is not good for the borderline individual and can lead to relapse into drugs or alcohol as well as self-destructive behavior. We also recommend a same sex sponsor. Sexual boundaries are an issue for many borderlines and we have seen some unfortunate relationships develop.

We feel strongly that individuals who are both chemically dependent and experience a borderline personality disorder initially require residential or inpatient treatment with a dual diagnosis approach. Treatment of this population requires high levels of structure and staff, special therapy skills, and provisions for responding rapidly to acting out and self-harm. We also feel strongly that any counselor working with these clients must be clearly in touch with his/her own family of origin issues. As part of their survivor skills, these individuals have become exquisitely sensitive to other people's "buttons" and will skillfully push them. Counselors who are vulnerable to enabling and rescuing, who insist that clients must get well or be considered bad, or who have weak boundaries themselves and who are easily taken advantage of by clients are asking for trouble when they work with this population. Key notions for managing a counseling relationship with a borderline personality disordered client include a "matter of fact, here-and-now attitude." We also "hope for the best, expect the worst, and settle for what we can get." Although borderline personality disordered clients can be difficult and a challenge to work with, many of them will improve with a dual diagnosis approach. Many of these clients will settle down after several years of turmoil with appropriate therapeutic interventions (4).

SUMMARY

Just as with major depression, many persons abusing or dependent on substances demonstrate behaviors suggestive of a personality disorder. This is especially true for antisocial traits. In most cases, these behaviors are a consequence of the substance use (16). However, some substance abusing/dependent individuals also have a coexisting personality disorder that requires simultaneous treatment. We have found the integrated mental health and recovery model described in this chapter useful in guiding them into a stable, clean, and sober life style.

REFERENCES

1. American Psychiatric Association.*Diagnostic and Statistical Manual of Mental Disorder, third edition*, revised. American Psychiatric Association, Washington, D.C., 1987.

2. Shuckit, M. A. The clinical implications of primary diagnostic groups among alcoholics. *Archives of General Psychiatry, 42,* 1043–1049, 1985.
3. Vaillant, G. *The Natural History of Alcoholism.* Harvard University Press, Cambridge, MA, 1983.
4. Nace, E. P. Alcoholism and other psychiatric disorders. In *The Treatment of Alcoholism.* Brunner/Mazel, New York, 1987.
5. Hesselbrock, M. N., Meyer, R. E., and Keener, J. J. Psychopathology in hospitalized alcoholics. *Archives of General Psychiatry, 42,* 1050–1055, 1985.
6. Liepman, M. R., and Nirenberg, T. D. Beginning treatment for alcohol problems. In D. C. Lewis and C. N. Williams (Eds.), *Providing Care for Children of Alcoholics: Clinical and Research Perspectives.* Health Communications, Pompano Beach, FL, 1986.
7. Liepman, M. R., Nirenberg, T. D., Porges, R. E., and Wartenburg, A. A. Depression associated with substance abuse. In O. G. Cameron (Ed.), *Presentations of Depression.* John Wiley & Sons, New York, 1987.
8. Zanarini M. C., and Gunderson, J. B. Childhood abuse common in borderline personality. *Clinical Psychiatry News, 6,* 1–2, 1987.
9. Rada, R. R. Sociopathy and alcoholism: Diagnostic and treatment implications. In W. H. Reid, (Ed.), *The Treatment of Antisocial Syndromes.* Van Nostrand and Rheinhold: New York, 1980.
10. Schukit, M. D. Genetic and clinical implications of alcoholism and affective disorder. *American Journal of Psychiatry, 143,* 140–147, 1986.
11. Perry, J. C. Depression in borderline personality disorder: Lifetime prevalence at interview and longitudinal course of symptoms. *American Journal of Psychiatry, 142 (1),* 15–21, 1985.
12. Bryer, J. B., Bernadette, A. N., Miller, J. B., et al. Childhood sexual abuse and physical abuse as factors in adult psychiatric illness. *American Journal of Psychiatry, 144,* 1426–1430, 1987.
13. Gartner, A. F., and Gartner, J. Borderline pathology in post-incest female adolescents. *The Menninger Bulletin, 52,* 101–113, 1988.
14. Lundberg, F. H., and Distad, L. J. Post-traumatic stress disorders in women who experienced childhood incest. *Child Abuse and Neglect, 9,* 329–334, 1985.
15. Bass, C., and Davis, L. *The Courage to Heal.* Harper & Row, New York, 1988.
16. Nathan, P. E. The addictive personality is the behavior of the addict. *Journal of Consulting and Clinical Psychology, 56(2),* 183–188, 1988.

7

Working with Adolescents

Treating the dual diagnosis adolescent presents a unique challenge to care providers. This chapter focuses on special issues of philosophy, assessment, and treatment that this population poses for the counselor and case manager, especially when a recovery model approach is used.

CASE EXAMPLE

The following case illustrates many of the issues involved in working with the adolescent who has a dual diagnosis. Janet was 13 years old when her disruptive school behavior and absenteeism became so severe that the school referred her to an outpatient drug and alcohol program for an evaluation. Janet, who had a history of sexual abuse by a neighbor and physical abuse by her alcoholic father, presented herself with fists clenched and head hung down during the assessment process. Janet was extremely resistant during the evaluation and minimized her use of drugs and alcohol. Janet discounted the school's concerns over her behavior and expressed a desire for people to just "get off my case." Janet's urine drug screen indicated heavy use of marijuana, in spite of Janet's fervent denial of drug use. She was referred to a local alcohol and drug residential treatment program for adolescents.

Although Janet's parents verbalized a desire to "get her help" they told staff that Janet was the family's only problem, and they refused to participate in family therapy. Janet felt extremely resentful toward her mother for placing her in the alcohol and drug program. In addition,

111

Janet had longstanding anger toward her mother. Janet felt that her mother loved her brother Bill more than she loved Janet. Janet also felt that her mother had failed to protect her from her abuse and that her mother had emotionally abandoned her. Janet's resentment deepened when the family refused therapy.

The staff in the residential program had difficulty with Janet when she refused to complete Step 1. Janet reported "I'm not powerless over anything, especially you jerkoffs." Frustrated and unsure how to proceed, the staff requested that a consulting psychologist do psychological testing on Janet. The psychologist was unable to convince Janet to complete the testing procedures. Janet's behavior continued to escalate. Some staff members felt that Janet was a negative influence on other youth in the program and that she should be discharged. Things came to a head when Janet threw a chair at a counselor who was trying to get Janet to take a time out in her room. Janet's parents were contacted and all parties felt it would be appropriate if she were transferred to a psychiatric hospital. Once she was hospitalized, staff working with a nurturing approach tried to get Janet to "open up," while other staff with a more confrontive approach gave her negative consequences for "manipulative behavior." Janet's psychiatrist felt that Janet was suicidal and that this should be the focus of the hospitalization, and he put Janet's drug abuse on the "back burner." Janet's parents met with the psychiatrist and shared their concern over Janet's problems. They expressed a desire to do whatever they could to help Janet except participate in family therapy. The family continued to express to hospital staff that Janet was the sole problem in their family.

Janet was discharged back to home after several months. She immediately relapsed and began drinking and smoking marijuana. Within 3 months, she began intravenous use of methamphetamine. She was rehospitalized at age 15 in a dual diagnosis program. The treatment plan this time focused on both Janet's substance abuse and her psychiatric problems. Janet was placed in a highly structured unit where the staff required her to finish psychological testing and to complete a Step 1 prior to receiving any privileges. Janet struggled with "surrender" for 72 hours but then completed her Step 1 and psychological testing.

She attended womens' issues groups for her sexual abuse issues (which had previously been unaddressed), and she received individual psychotherapy with a psychologist who had expertise in working with dual diagnosis adolescents. She had 2 hours a day of chemical dependency counseling. She continued working the steps of Alcoholics Anonymous, using specialized step work designed for dually diagnosed clients, and attended A.A. and N.A. meetings both in the hospital and in the community. Janet was discharged with a home behavior contract specifying expectations and consequences for problem behaviors. This contract had been the focus of 6 weeks of family meetings, which were a requirement of the program. Once home, she attended outpatient counseling, aftercare, and family therapy. At the time of this writing, Janet has 24 months of continuous sobriety and is no longer acting out and suicidal.

In Janet's case the use of a primary–secondary model, with one problem given priority over the other, resulted in unsuccessful treatment. Treating her within a coexisting disorders model appeared to work better. Managing Janet's acting out, dealing with her sexual and physical abuse issues, and involving her family also proved crucial.

SPECIAL CONCERNS

Even more so than with adults, the counselor or case manager attempting to work with dually diagnosed adolescents has little literature and research to guide his/her efforts. Assessing and treating adolescents for either substance abuse or a psychiatric disorder are relatively new and developing fields (see Ref. 1). This is even more the case for adolescents with *both* a substance abuse *and* a psychiatric disorder. Once again, we have found it useful to integrate mental health notions and recovery models to help us treat such adolescents. Whereas Chapter 2 discussed our manner of blending these approaches and the associated issues in some detail, working with adolescents with dual diagnoses from within such a framework can raise additional concerns.

Using a Twelve Step recovery model for the adolescent abusing or dependent on chemicals sometimes raises certain issues. Rather than seeing an adolescent as exhibiting the signs and symptoms of the disease of chemical dependency, one view is that the chemical use is a part of normal adolescent rebellion, a reflection of the emotional turbulence of this age and part of the search for an identity. Experimentation with chemicals is seen as part and parcel of growing up. The difficulty of establishing progression of use over time lends support to this stance. Influenced by the "symptom-of-something-else" model of chemical abuse and dependency, someone with this point of view poses the question, "How do you know these adolescents can never drink successfully, and what about all the other problems they're showing?" Another concern involves the practice of encouraging the chemically abusing or dependent adolescent to adopt the label of "alcoholic" or "addict." The fear is that these adolescents, seeking to establish a personal identity as part of this stage of their development, will incorporate a seemingly negative concept into their sense of who they are in the world.

Another objection that we've encountered involves the issue of adolescent consent for treatment. Adolescents deserve the same rights as adults and sometimes families and cooperating service systems have unjustly locked up adolescents and treated them against their will, according to this stance. Adolescents forced into treatment are victims of scapegoating by the family and are being stripped of their rights without due process. A related argument is that, unless the adolescent accepts the need for treatment, therapy will fail. Finally, some professionals argue that the family conflict often present among the members of the adolescent's family system points to the need for working from within a family therapy framework. Taken as an exclusive approach the priority must then be on putting the parents back in charge, resolving conflicts, and establishing appropriate interactions among family members. The dual diagnosis adolescent's multiple, interacting problems often intensify these debates by seeming to provide evidence for all these concerns.

Some adolescents who abuse chemicals and get into trouble as youths go on to be reasonably well-adjusted adults with no evidence of a progressive addiction. Families of adolescents abusing and dependent on chemicals do sometimes have a history of family problems *prior* to the onset of significant chemical use by their child. Families and service systems have sometimes made the adolescent a scapegoat and trampled on the adolescent's rights. There are, however, other aspects to these issues.

For most adolescents most of the time, life is fairly normal and without significant crises. The myth of the stormy adolescence is only a myth. Occasional moodiness and high jinks are part of this period in life, but anything beyond this is not typical and chemical use by adolescents is problematic. Chemicals such as marijuana can interfere with hormonal and neurological development. This is a crucial issue for adolescents as they progress through a stage of rapid physical maturation and are vulnerable to chemical disruption of normal maturation processes. Youth who abuse chemicals can also experience interference with their emotional and psychological development. Significant chemical usage interferes with the development of a positive, prosocial identity. The involvement with chemicals can lead to an identity crystallized around being a "stoner" and having antisocial values stressing dishonesty, the rip-off, and immediate gratification. Membership in socially marginal groups, failure in school, and conflict at home do not lay a good foundation for future success. Exploring intimacy is also not possible when under the influence. The adolescent abusing drugs is not available emotionally and is likely to have problems coping with the complexities of establishing and maintaining close relationships. The implication of all this? We restate our guideline that what causes a problem is a problem. Adolescence in and of itself does not cause problems. Chemical use often does. We would rather be safe than sorry and encourage adolescents to develop chemical-free life styles.

Adolescents have rights, including the right of due process, and the adolescent willing to admit having a drug problem is certainly an easier client, if a rare one. However, our laws recognize that adolescents are not adults and these laws require parental or guardian consent for major decisions such as getting married, entering the armed services, and signing contracts. Society has also determined that adolescents are not yet capable of making mature decisions when it comes to voting or drinking alcohol. Accidents, murders, and acquired immune deficiency syndrome are also complications of chemical involvement even for adolescents. We have treated adolescents brain-damaged from a car wreck where the driver was intoxicated. Gang membership is increasing, and drug use and dealing are a primary focus for these gangs. Fourteen-year-olds are shooting each other. Life styles involving promiscuity and intravenous drug use can expose a youth to the AIDS virus. We have treated 12-year-old prostitutes who shot crack intravenously who had contracted the AIDS virus.

Trying gently to convince a child whose brain is under the influence and who is in denial that she needs treatment for addiction is likely to end in failure. Consider also the plight of the parents trying to deal with their out-of-control youngster. We watched one desperate family carry their daughter in a sleeping bag secured with duct tape and assisted by two burly uncles. Good parents, they had reached the end of their rope as their runaway, needle-using, promiscuous daughter refused to listen to "reason." The parents of these adolescents are in a double bind. They are responsible for the actions of their child and for their growth and development. But some state laws do not allow parents to access mental health or chemical dependency treatment without the child's consent. With parental or guardian consent, we are comfortable treating the unwilling adolescent and have found their ability to obtain sobriety and stability equal to that of their counterparts who entered treatment willingly (also see Chapter 9).

Accepting the label of alcoholic or addict can empower the adolescent. We feel that the initial acceptance of their addiction is demonstrated in their willingness to identify with the recovering addict/

alcoholic label. Within the recovery framework, youth can came to believe they are "sick getting well," not "bad getting better." These adolescents gain a prosocial group of peers and older, more mature adults through the fellowship of Alcoholics or Narcotics Anonymous. Youth accepting the label develop ethical and spiritual values that include honesty, conscious contact with a power greater than themselves, and dedication to helping others as part of their Twelve Step recovery program.

We discuss the role of the family in greater depth in the next chapter. Chemical use does cause family conflict or exacerbate existing difficulties. Whether cause, effect, or both, in our experience and the experience of others (2), abstinence is necessary for successful family work and, analogous to the coexisting models, simultaneous treatment of the child and family difficulties is necessary for successful outcomes. Families torn apart by the devastation of a mentally ill substance abusing youth need time to heal and the guidance and support of a trained family therapist to help the family in its own journey of recovery.

ASSESSMENT

Most of the assessment principles discussed in Chapters 3 and 4 are relevant to adolescent assessments. There are, however, issues unique to adolescents. Looking at systems problems is a key way to assess chemical dependency in adolescents, including dual diagnosis adolescents. School is an important system because this is a place where the adolescent spends 6 to 7 hours a day, faces work-like demands for performance, and finds friends. School is a microcosm of society. Teachers often notice the effects of drugs and alcohol on a child's performance and are often the first adults to notice a problem. Memory impairment and reduction in abstract thinking are common in the adolescent substance abuser. As use continues, the youth becomes apathetic and disinterested in studies. The youth fails to turn in assignments and is ill-prepared for tests and reports. The youth begins a pattern of tardiness and then absenteeism. Extracurricular activities drop off. An athletic child decides that track is now "boring," and all the participants are "jocks" and "nerds." A young thespian may feel drama club is now "stupid." Old friends are gradually replaced by new "cool" friends who also are drinking and drug abusing. School officials often develop checklists for identifying the drug abusing youth and recommending a formal chemical abuse assessment (see Appendix 2 for an example). Behaviors observed may include the following: tardiness, absenteeism, apathy, sleepiness in class, moodiness, negative attitude, change in friends, lost interest in school activities, incomplete assignments, and change in dress.

Families are, of course, our "home" system. The drug- or alcohol-abusing adolescent becomes increasingly uncomfortable in an environment where adults are trying to set limits on his or her behavior and where adults expect communication and honesty. Family members will note such problematic behaviors as loss of interest in school activities, isolation in room, and money missing from their wallets in the adolescent abusing drugs, including the dual diagnosis adolescent. Appendix 3 has a home behavior checklist for parents that pinpoints typical problem behaviors.

Pinpointing classic signs of chemical dependency can be difficult with adolescents. Although we have seen 11-year-olds requiring alcohol detox, dramatic withdrawal symptoms as well as physical problems are relatively uncommon with adolescents. Standard notions of progression are difficult to use as criteria of chemical dependence as well. Adolescents often have episodic, binge-like use patterns instead of gradual increases in use. One useful tip to remember is that a youth who is becoming more and more preoccupied with use, and who is expanding the variety of chemicals used, demonstrates a kind of progression. Remember also that adolescents can show another kind of rapid progression involving high levels of chemical intake in one session. Peer-influenced games focused on rapid intake, such as chugging shots and shooting beers, contribute to this progression in a number of adolescents.

Adolescents do evidence loss of control with a violation of their rules for use. Asking the question, "Have you ever drunk or used more than planned" is relevant for both adults and adolescents. Adolescents develop their own rules for drinking and using such as "I'll never use hard drugs." When they break these rules it shows loss of control. Adolescents will also exhibit denial and thinking errors. Blaming others and minimizing problems are two common thinking errors.

The discussion in Chapter 4 about establishing the psychiatric diagnosis for dual diagnosis clients is pertinent to working with dual diagnosis adolescents. Base-rate issues, the ability of chemical use to mimic psychiatric disorders, and the need for a comprehensive assessment apply to this population.

We have found that troubled adolescents tend to express their difficulties in behavior. Adolescents often are still developing their abilities to reason abstractly and use words to express and deal with their impulses and conflicts. Adolescents also continue to feel dependent on powerful others for their needs and feel conflict about expressing their needs in direct ways. When in trouble, adolescents are more likely than adults to act rather than think and to rebel rather than negotiate. The majority of dual diagnosis adolescents present with some kind of acting out behavior no matter what the coexisting disorder. Many dual diagnosis youths harbor deep anger and resentment toward family members and authority figures. Parents, especially those who had been neglectful or abusive, are objects of intense feeling. For youth who *act out*, defiance of parents, running away, threatening and assaultive behavior, vandalism, and promiscuity are common. Youth who *act in* can become self-destructive and suicidal. Many of these adolescents engage in self-mutilating behavior by cutting themselves with knives and razor blades. Using drugs and alcohol further disrupts effective coping and adds fuel to the fire of family dysfunction. The adolescents then gravitate toward peers like themselves who are learning that chemicals kill the pain. And so the problem escalates.

A common assessment dilemma facing the evaluator is distinguishing among "normal" adolescent behavior, behavioral difficulties resulting from chemical use alone, and the acting out of the antisocial adolescent who is also chemically dependent. Early substance abuse appears common among individuals with an antisocial personality disorder (see Ref. 3). Table 9 outlines differences that we have observed among these three groups. When reviewing the table, the reader will note that the behavior of the "normal" adolescent is greatly intensified when describing the "drug abusing" adolescent. Drug-abusing adolescents begin to display life problems such as school problems, family problems, and some legal problems. The substance abusing youth has also begun to display thinking errors such as rationalizing and blaming. These youths use these thinking errors to justify their continued use of drugs in spite of growing evidence that drugs are becoming a problem. These youths still feel guilt and remorse over negative and harmful behavior but use drugs and alcohol to rid themselves of emotions. Antisocial adolescents, in comparison, have long rid themselves of empathy, passion, and remorse. Their thinking errors are continuous and their behavior is blatantly antisocial.

Another assessment dilemma for the evaluator is distinguishing between the true antisocial and the borderline personality disordered adolescent who appears antisocial. Many adolescents who have experienced serious physical and/or sexual abuse at the hands of adults act out as a way to deal with the pain of these experiences and protect themselves from further harm. Readers will find the material discussed in Chapter 5 regarding the antisocial and borderline personality disorders relevant to this task. A comprehensive assessment, with

TABLE 9
Characteristics of "Normal" Adolescent, Antisocial Adolescent, and
Drug-Abusing Adolescent

Area	"Normal" adolescent	"Drug-abusing" adolescent	"Antisocial" adolescent
Affect	Moodiness	Drastic mood swings, guilty anger	Angry and controlling or calm, smooth, and charming
World view	"I should be able to do anything I want to" "I feel like I am not as good at things as I would like to be" "If I steal I might get caught, then people would know I'm a thief"	"I've done some bad things and I feel guilty" "If I don't stay on top of things people will find out I'm bad" "I have to steal to get money—besides all my friends do it"	"I'm cool—you don't matter unless you have something I want" "It's not bad unless you get caught" "You're a fool and deserve to be ripped off"
Presenting problem	Moodiness, feeling insecure, unliked	School problems, family conflict, change of friends, drastic mood swings, lying, legal problems: theft, breaking and entering	Violent behavior, violent crimes, rageful outbursts Families and others injured and like wreckage following the trail of the antisocial
Social functioning	Good achievement, positive peer group, interest or outside hobby	Current problems, things growing progressively worse	Excellent functioning, e.g., class president, in charge of everything, smooth talker, or poor functioning, numerous law violations, volatile relationships
Motivation	Autonomy, peer identification	To return to previous positive functioning, acceptance of peers	To win—be right; control, seek stimulation/excitement—short-term
Defenses	Isolation, minimizing, blame	Lying, manipulation, increased use of thinking errors	Con, pure, and continues use of thinking errors

special attention to the elevation of scales 6 and 8 on the MMPI, will help to make this determination. We have found that the higher these two scales are, the more likely it is that the antisocial behavior is the result of the trauma of abuse in the absence of psychotic symptoms.

Some adolescents have an early-onset bipolar or schizophrenic disorder. These are often difficult to detect, especially when chemical use is also present, but they need to be considered if there are signs and symptoms justifying this concern. Sometimes a carefully monitored trial of medication is the only way to confirm these possibilities and treatment professionals should consider this if other behavioral interventions have failed. The evaluator trying to determine if an adolescent abusing chemicals also has a coexisting psychiatric disorder can attend to the quality of the adolescent's presenting problems and associated signs and symptoms. The dual diagnosis adolescent will show more intense problems and these problems will have a different "flavor" than the troubles of the adolescent with "only" a chemical use problem. The "damaged" antisocial adolescent, for example, will have a history of cruel and very destructive acts even when not intoxicated. These acts include fire setting and animal torture. The early-onset adolescent schizophrenic will be socially isolated and not even have drug-using peers and will also show ongoing bizarre thinking and behavior. Table 10 lists typical presenting problems and signs and symptoms that we have observed with dual diagnosis adolescents with certain coexisting disorders.

Evaluators also need to be alert to subtle organic deficits such as a seizure disorder expressed in intermittent explosive episodes, attention-deficit disorder with or without hyperactivity, and subtle learning disabilities. Adolescents with such subtle organic deficits are at high risk for problematic chemical use (see Ref. 4). Besides their impulsivity, their experience of being different and failing in school leave them vulnerable to the seductive call of socially marginal peer groups and the pleasant effects of chemicals. When adolescents have any history of inhalant use or any long-term use of other chemicals, evaluation for an organic mental disorder is also indicated. Neurological and neuropsychological evaluation can be helpful here in assessing these organic difficulties.

The prevalence of dually disordered adolescents is unknown. One report (5) indicated a third of adolescents admitted to this inpatient program had dual diagnosis, with various depressive disorders, conduct disorders, and attention deficit syndrome the most frequent coexisting disorder. Research using strict procedures and in different settings is needed.

TREATMENT

We generally use the same approaches for dual diagnosis adolescents that we use for dual diagnosis adults. We advocate simultaneous treatment for coexisting disorders and use a combination of mental

TABLE 10
Common Signs, Symptoms, and Problems Observed Among Certain Groups of Dual Diagnosis Adolescents

Adolescents with a coexisting conduct or antisocial personality disorder

Presenting problems
  Stealing
  Legal violations
  Thrill-seeking element in acting out
  Arson
  Truancy
  Fights at school
  Failing grades
  Problems with authority
  Sexually exploitive relationships/sexual offending
  Severe family conflict, physical and verbal fighting
Thinking
  Chronic use of thinking errors
  Intense denial, projection, and blame
  Strong need for "look good" image
  Win/lose mind set
  Attitude of entitlement
  Self-absorbed
  Short attention span
Affect
  Empty and cold
  Mock or faking of "feelings" when needed
  Lack of remorse
  Charming and slick
  Depressed when caught
  Angry intimidation
Interpersonal relationships
  Wreckage following parasitic relationships
  Shallow and self-serving
  Strong need for control
  Abusive and demanding
Patterns of drug use
  "If it feels good, do it twice"
  The more, the better
  Polysubstance use, preference for amphetamine, crack, coke, and alcohol

Adolescents with a coexisting borderline personality disorder

Presenting problems
  Self-harm, self-mutilation
  Suicide attempts; drug, alcohol overdoses
  Cruelty to other children
  Angry attacks on others, unprovoked
  Fire setting
  Cult involvement
  Problems with authority

(Continued)

TABLE 10 *(Continued)*

Thinking
  Black and white
  Numerous thinking errors
  Devaluation
  Preoccupation with pain and death
  Negative world view
  Get you before you get me
  Help me! But you can't!
Affect
  Self-loathing
  Anger towards self and others
  Extremely volatile
  Depression
Interpersonal relationships
  Hot/cold
  Too intense, too quick
  Love/hate
  Enmeshment
  Overidentification
  Charming and seductive
  Lack of consistent peer group
Substance abuse problems
  Episodic substance abuse
  Polydrug use: methamphetamine, LSD, alcohol

Adolescents with a coexisting bipolar disorder

Presenting problems
  Sexual promiscuity
  Highly impulsive
  Hyperactive
  Legal problems
  Runaway
  Truancy
Thinking
  Use of thinking errors
  Rapid thoughts
  Short attention span
  Easily distracted
  Grandiose
  Delusional
Affect
  Elation/mania
  Irrationality
  Agitation
  Depression/anger
Interpersonal
  Strong need for social interactions
  Brief

(Continued)

TABLE 10 *(Continued)*

Brief
Intense quality
Quantity of relationships
Seductive
Substance abuse
Polydrug: amphetamines, alcohol, pot, coke, crack

Adolescent with a coexisting schizophrenic disorder

Presenting problems
Psychosis
Depression
Suicide attempts
Bizarre behavior
Erratic violent behavior
Thinking
Crazy, weird quality
Psychotic
Concrete
Paranoid
Affect
Flat, empty quality
Pacing agitation
Depression, withdrawn
Interpersonal
Isolative
Separate from group
Vacuous quality
Lack of peer group
Drug abuse
Polydrug: hallucinogenic, alcohol, pot

health approaches and modified step work. The step work in Appendix 1 for schizophrenic, bipolar, and organic mental disorders and for antisocial and borderline personalities is generally quite appropriate for use with similarly diagnosed adolescents. Although we are more conservative in recommending medication and insist on a trial of behavioral interventions, we are comfortable using nonaddictive medication if careful assessment indicates this to be appropriate.

However, there are some special considerations when treating dual diagnosis adolescents. When involved in chemical dependency counseling we have found that Twelve Step work is most helpful. Step 1 work involves surrender and the realization of powerlessness. Adolescents need to accept that their drinking and using are out of control and unmanageable. Counselors should remember, however, that dual diagnosis adolescents, like all adolescents, live very much in the present. Dating a partner for 3 weeks constitutes a serious relationship. Adolescents believe they will live forever. An hour can seem like a lifetime. In addition, adolescents have often achieved very little compared to a 40-year-old adult and consequently often feel they have little to lose. Counselors are more likely to be successful if they keep these issues in mind.

Addicted youth do not respond like adult alcoholics to discussions regarding health, role performance, family, and death. The statement "you will die if you keep drinking" gets the attention of most adult substance abusers. An adolescent substance abuser may respond, "everyone dies, plus it could take me 20 to 30 more years of partying before that happens!" Counselors need to focus on current instances of negative consequences and instances of negative outcomes likely in the short run. Today and this week are often appropriate time frames. For the adolescent overwhelmed with the idea of never drinking or using again, focusing on "one day at a time" and abstaining "just for today" is useful. The dual diagnosis youth can often acknowledge how much emotional turmoil he/she is in—this affords the opportunity to point out that drugs are no longer working and to offer sobriety as an option for pain reduction.

Step 2 with the adolescent presents some special concerns. "Came to believe a power greater than ourselves could restore us to sanity" requires abstract thinking combined with faith, both of which pose difficulties for the adolescent. We work with youth on helping them identify people and situations that indicate that their life is improving since discontinuing alcohol and drug abuse. There is a famous story told around the table of Twelve Step meetings. It is known as the "Eskimo story." This story highlights Step 2's requirement of faith and higher power. We often tell this story to adolescents when helping them understand the concept of faith.

Two men were sitting alone waiting for a bus. One of the men wore the collar of a Catholic priest. The other man turned to the priest and said "I once prayed to your God to save my life and he failed me!" The priest smiled and said, "Tell me, my son, of your prayer." The man went on to tell how he had been lost in the arctic cold of Alaska, he had no food or shelter and was certain he was going to die. In his last breath, he begged God to save him from death. The priest smiled and said, "But son, God did not fail you. You are alive." The man replied, "God didn't do anything. Some Eskimo showed me the way out."

We try to help the adolescent understand that the higher power works through people and that "Eskimos" are everywhere helping us when we most need help. We ask the youth to make lists of the "Eskimos" or people who have been helpful to him personally. We discuss these "helpers" in group counseling.

Step 3 requires the adolescent to "turn [his/her] will and life over to the care of God as [he/she] understand[s] Him." Counselors need to help the adolescent find an appropriate higher power. We discourage youth from choosing heavy metal rock music groups, doorknobs, or other unlikely sources of spiritual contact. Most often youth choose the A.A. group itself if they are uncomfortable with a more traditional view of God or have difficulty with the abstract concept of higher power.

Because many dual diagnosis adolescents present with intense out-of-control behavior and are so influenced by negative peers, we feel that effective adolescent treatment initially requires a residential or inpatient milieu that is guided and controlled by staff. Staff must establish and enforce prorecovery behavior and develop and promote positive peers. This is most easily done in a residential or inpatient program. We are willing to try outpatient treatment with a dual diagnosis adolescent who is motivated for recovery, who is not endangering his/her own welfare or that of the family, and who has an intact positive support system. We will often make a contingency plan with the adolescent and the family that if the youth fails in the outpatient setting then the youth will enter a more intensive setting. However, in our experience, many dual diagnosis adolescents need to begin their recovery in the more intensive setting.

A milieu is more likely to be positive if there is a status or level system with immediate consequences for behavior, both positive and negative. A key prorecovery behavior to promote in adolescents is the challenging of negative behavior and thinking (thinking errors) demonstrated by others. Besides harnessing the power of their peers, this helps reduce the number of "enablers" who passively watch the "good kids" confront the "bad kids." Another useful strategy is to reduce the privileges of upper-level adolescents if lower-level adolescents act out. This promotes an alliance between staff and the upper-level adolescents.

A prorecovery milieu will also forbid the wearing of clothes or symbols that point to identification with antisocial, drug-using groups. Wearing Satanic tee shirts or sporting pink hairdos only serves to maintain a negative identity and blocks surrender and acceptance of the new identity as a recovering alcoholic or addict. Similarly, staff should forbid war stories. As nearly as possible the milieu should encourage prosocial dress and behavior, and provide a schedule of daily activities resembling the real world of the adolescent. This includes provisions for school time, family time, and play.

Work with the various systems of the adolescent is essential. Chapter 8 discusses family work in more detail. But sometimes return to the family is impossible. In cases where abuse is present or where the parents' alcoholism is so acute that the adolescent's recovery would be jeopardized if sent home, then alternate placement becomes necessary. If sexual or physical abuse is identified during the course of treatment, we *always* report it to the appropriate authorities. We believe the secrecy of use must be broken if healing is to begin. We always put the safety of the child first. It would be wonderful if all adolescents had an Aunt Irene or a special relative who could provide an extended family resource to the child when immediate family members are not available. Halfway houses and group homes for adolescents, where staying clean and sober is a focus, are also extremely helpful in these cases. Sadly, in most cases, neither of these options is available. Underfunded public agencies have stretched their resources to the limit. If the adolescent is 16 or 17, early emancipation may be an option. In this case we assist the adolescent in completing a GED, getting and keeping a job, and finding a place to live. For those too young to emancipate and who have no alternative, we have attempted to achieve psychological emancipation despite unavoidable residence in the dysfunctional family home. We help the youngster understand the difference between his/her problem and his/her parents' problems. We encourage such youngsters to identify safe and supportive people and places, such as a friendly neighbor, an A.A. meeting, or the local church, that they can use for support and times out from their family. Occasionally this works, but often the youth relapses. We have often seen these youth become reinvolved with chemicals and even return to the streets. Their sobriety did not provide a roof over their heads and food in their stomach nor meet their safety and esteem needs. We are hopeful that funding may soon become available for youth halfway houses to prevent these tragedies.

Coordination with schools is extremely important. Besides providing excellent collateral data, the program staff and school personnel can work on developing remedial school programs designed to meet any special educational needs the adolescent may have. Many schools offer groups supporting sobriety and providing prorecovery peers. Schools can also monitor progress and detect a relapse. Probation officers, child protective service workers, and other involved service providers can serve similar functions. By having this group of people work together as a team and become involved in all phases of care the chances of a successful outcome will increase. These other systems can also provide contingencies for enforcing treatment plans such as revocation of parole and return to a supervised living situation if the youth relapses. The dual diagnosis adolescent will benefit from all the services and strategies for preventing relapse as discussed in Chapter 9; particularly important is that he/she learn to have fun and resocialize with a clean and sober peer group.

The dually diagnosed adolescent presents a multitude of problems and behaviors that challenge the treatment professional. However, as with all adolescents, their energy, honesty, direct expression of feelings, idealism, and rapid response to environmental change can make them interesting and rewarding clients.

REFERENCES

1. McDermott, J. F., Werry, J., Petti, T., et al. Anxiety disorders of childhood and adolescence. In T.B. Karasu (Ed.), *Treatments of Psychiatric Disorders*. American Psychiatric Association, Washington, D.C., pp. 401–446, 1989.
2. Kaufman, E. Family therapy with adolescent substance abusers. In M. A. Miriken and S. C. Koman (Eds.), *Handbook of Adolescent and Family Therapy*. Gardner Press, New York, pp. 245–254, 1985.
3. Hesselbrock, M. N., Meyer, R. E., and Keener, J. J. Psychopathology in hospitalized alcoholics. *Archives of General Psychiatry*, *42*, pp. 1050–1055, 1985.
4. Donnelly, M. Attention deficit hyperactivity disorder and conduct disorder. In T. B. Karasu (Ed.), *Treatments of Psychiatric Disorders*. American Psychiatric Association, Washington, D.C., pp. 365–398, 1989.
5. Chamberlain, R. E., and Tarr, J. E. Identifying chemical dependency is not enough. *Adolescent Counselor*, *2(3)*, 25, 1989.

8

Working with Families

Chemical abuse and psychiatric disorders both have serious negative effects on all family members. Whether cause or effect, these problems seriously disrupt family members, both the identified patient and his or her significant others. Families with a dually diagnosed member experience at least twice the problems of those with a family member with one disorder. Clinical attention to the family is crucial. This chapter discusses some of the issues facing the service provider working with the families of dual diagnosis clients and presents some approaches for working with these families.

THE DYSFUNCTIONAL FAMILY

Families are a major focal point in an individual's life. Whether defined as the nuclear family, the extended kinship network, or significant others, families provide the setting for the individual's most frequent and extended contacts with others. These contacts also have an emotional intensity and weight greater than all others. Families are a primary source for the satisfaction of a person's physiological safety, belongingness, and self-esteem needs. Whereas no family is perfect, most families manage to function reasonably well. However, introduce a psychiatric disorder, compound this with chemical dependency, and the best of families can become dysfunctional and off balance.

To have success in assisting the dually disordered person to achieve stability and sobriety, including the family in treatment is generally important. Family members can make either a negative contribution

129

toward the maintenance and exacerbation of the client's problems or become a key to the solution. Writers in the chemical dependency treatment field, for example, have done an excellent job of identifying the role of enabling family members (see Ref. 1). These family members rescue the client from the negative consequences of his/her chemical use and, despite their best intentions, inadvertently reinforce the problem. Most professionals agree that family therapy is a useful part of the treatment of individuals with a substance abuse and/or psychiatric disorder. However, many family approaches exist (see Refs. 2–5), and although the evidence is growing there is little firm research to document the best approach for different kinds of clients and families; additionally, results are sometimes not straightforward (see Refs. 6,7).

We embrace a genuine systems view that acknowledges the mutual interaction of all family members and the evolving nature of the situation over time in our work with families. A family member has a problem, and the rest of the family responds in an attempt to cope with it. Sometimes the attempts to manage the problem actually make things worse. Maybe young Jack got in with a bad, drug using crowd because of parental conflict. Or perhaps having a drug-abusing, out-of-control child has led to arguments and a parental failure to intervene. Maybe Jill started to develop problems as her parents pushed her to succeed in college and live independently. Or perhaps Jill's problems, later diagnosed as schizophrenia, caused her parent's concern and led them to overinvolve themselves in her life. Rather than an *either/or* framework, the more appropriate view when dealing with these families is an *either/and* framework. This framework also minimizes blaming and scapegoating of any family member.

Many models exist for describing the dysfunction of disrupted families. George Howard, M.A., a colleague of ours, presents a model with two axes that we find useful. The first axis has the endpoints of chaos versus rigidity. The second axis has the endpoints of enmeshment versus disengagement. Putting the two together results in this schema:

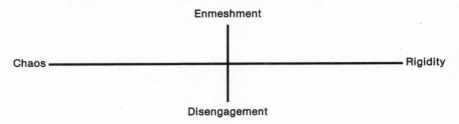

All families fall somewhere on the coordinates of these axes. Unhealthy families tend toward the extremes in their functioning. Chaotic families are unpredictable in their behavior, with seemingly inconsistent rules governing their interactions. Rigid families, in contrast, respond in overly determined ways and are inflexible in their responses even when the situation calls for exceptions or new rules. The members of disengaged families have little interaction and keep emotional distance. These families resemble neighbors living in large, anonymous apartment buildings. The members of enmeshed families, on the other hand, interact too intensely and have poor boundaries. If one member sneezes, the rest of the family gets a cold. The chaotic/disengaged family has abandoned each other and the members are in crisis. The rigid/enmeshed family typically has a pseudonormal appearance, and the rigid/disengaged family is no longer a family.

Members of dysfunctional families strive to maintain a balance between the extremes of these axes in the face of problematic behavior. But typically their responses are reactive, represent the extreme of the other axis, and inadvertently reinforce the problem. The more severe the family, the farther from the center they are. The goal of treatment then becomes one of moving the family toward the center of these axes through the use of consistent but flexible rules and caring, but clear, interactions with appropriate boundaries. This goal , together with the presenting problems of the family, helps determine the objectives of treatment.

THE DYSFUNCTIONAL FAMILY WITH A DUAL DIAGNOSIS MEMBER

Tolstoy remarked that all happy families are alike but that unhappy families are unhappy in unique ways. We feel, in contrast, that there are many creative ways to be a happy family but that unhappy families are remarkably and distressingly alike. Writers such as Melodie Beattie (1), Janet Woititz (8), and Claudia Black (9) have written extensively about the effects of alcohol and drug use on family members. Other writers such as Salvador Minuchin have written about the presentation of families with a member with a psychiatric disorder (2). We find remarkable similarities in their descriptions, and, in our experience, their notions apply to dual diagnosis families, with one exception. Everything tends to be worse for the dual diagnosis family.

A key theme in the dysfunctional family with a dual diagnosis member is the attempt to control the uncontrollable. The dual diagnosis individual is unable to simply say, "Well, today I think I'll be clean and sober and exhibit normal mood, thinking, and behavior." If he/she could, he/she would not be in your office receiving these diagnoses. Similarly, attempts by family members to get the dual diagnosis individual to function normally and to keep a normal family atmosphere will often not work. Family members who strongly demand high performance levels from a member with only schizophrenia, for example, increase relapse rates even when the individual is on medication (10). Some families apply their control efforts in an inconsistent and chaotic fashion. If the families members are enmeshed, this can lead to periodic crises marked by arguments, running away, battering, and other forms of domestic violence. As the family relents, a period of seeming calm follows. This is temporary, however, and the cycle restarts itself. If disengaged, everyone does his/her own thing and tends to drift apart. We remember the parents of one person, diagnosed as both alcoholic and schizophrenic, who would tear up his room and terrorize the neighbors. The parents state that they would sometimes ask their son to be good or call the police. Recently the parents had moved into the basement and begun using the back door to avoid arguments. This allowed their son to do as he wished.

Some families apply their control efforts in a rigid, "no exceptions" way. If disengaged, this often results in complete abandonment of the dual diagnosis client. We are impressed by the large number of adult dual diagnosis clients who have little or no contact with family members. The family returns letters unopened, hangs up on the phone, and never remembers birthdays or holidays. If engaged, the family often appears pseudonormal. Claudia Black (9) has written extensively of rules often seen in unhealthy families and their impact in the alcoholic family. These rules also characterize the dual diagnosis family in our experience. These rules are:

1. *Don't talk.* it's not safe or okay to discuss with each other or anyone outside the family what is going on. The belief is developed that, if family members just pretend everything is all right and don't rock the boat, somehow everything will work out just fine. Because problems are never discussed openly, the family members begin to doubt their own perceptions. The member may wonder if "maybe I'm just imagining this, maybe he hasn't been drinking." Self-doubt soars, insecurity builds, and self-esteem plummets.

2. *Don't trust.* Family members learn that they can't predict the behavior of the impaired member. Promises are routinely made and broken, and expectations change constantly. The family members begin to develop a lack of confidence both in themselves and in people around them. They feel as if they have no one they can count on who can give them the unconditional love they desperately seek.

3. *Don't feel.* Feelings are painful and scary. The family member learns it's not wise to share feelings with others. They may even be told "Don't be a cry-baby," or " You need to toughen up." Feelings are perceived as a weakness. People who display feelings easily are seen as "sick" or "messed up." The feelings experienced by family members are often so overwhelming that they suspect that they are "crazy" if they share their emotional turmoil with others. They are concerned that they will be labeled sick or bad, ensuring that no one will ever want them or love them. Keeping feelings "under control" is a struggle that can often be a life-long battle.

We have often found an enabling family member to be in these sorts of families. Typically this is a well-intentioned spouse, but it may be a parent or older child. The enabling family member is the one who attempts to control the behavior of the dual diagnosis individual while rescuing that person from the negative consequences of his/her behavior. The enabling relative's intent is to help but, ironically, his/her efforts often make things worse. Perhaps he/she is pouring alcohol down the sink or removing all weapons from the home. Maybe he/she is hiding car keys from the intoxicated individual. Perhaps he/she bails the person out of jail or continues to give money for rent and medication to the person , who then spends it on irrational purchases or alcohol. With this support, both the dual diagnosis client and the family members get deeper and deeper into trouble and pain.

Steinglass (11) has identified other issues important to keep in mind when working with the family with a member who is abusing or dependent on chemicals. We feel these also apply to many families with a dually diagnosed member. Psychoactive drugs negatively impact a person's functioning at the physiological level as well as other levels, and the client must achieve abstinence for long-term success with the family. We also attempt to get other family members to remain abstinent for a period of time in order to support the recovery of the client and to help assess substance abuse issues in other family members. Chemical dependency and many psychiatric disorders also have both a genetic component and a learned one, and several generations of the family may have had members evidencing these disorders. Careful assessment of other family members to identify either of these disorders or the consequences of having lived with a parent or spouse with one of these disorders is important. Many individuals with chemical dependency or a psychiatric disorder cycle through stages ranging from stable to acute. Family members can feel severely stressed by the unpredictable nature of these cycles, can see the client as having control over his/her behavior, or can believe that no further work is necessary because everything is now calm.

TREATMENT APPROACHES

Both the client and his/her family members have their own battle scars from their fight with chemical dependency and the psychiatric disorder. Both the family member identified as "sick" and other family members are now clients and all need to enter recovery.

Just as with the client, early and late recovery have different goals. Early recovery has the goal of family stability where the emphasis is on a happy medium between chaos and rigidity and the setting of appropriate boundaries to avoid the extremes of enmeshment and disengagement. Later in recovery the emphasis on the family is more on growth and the enhancement of their relationships. In our experience, the "outside-in strategy" mentioned in Chapter 2 also applies to families. Family work that leaps into in-depth, emotional processing early on is bound to fail. First things first with families as well as the identified client. We provide safety and structure prior to exploring painful feelings.

We have found the following approaches useful in early recovery. We also tend to prefer to work first with family members only at this stage if the client is still unstable. The client has his/her own work to do and family members need to feel safe to change without the fear of confrontation and a temper outburst from the client.

EDUCATION

The objective of this intervention is to reframe the presenting problems, validate and support the family, and motivate them for further change. Didactic information groups where families learn about both chemical dependency and the psychiatric disorder, combined with sharing information and the impact these personal experiences have had on family members are crucial. Telling the secret, learning to attribute the damage to the twin illnesses, and finding out they are not alone are powerful experiences for many family members.

SUPPORT GROUPS

The objective here is to provide education, emotional support, and a start on working through the issues facing the family. Al-Anon, Alateen, and similar groups are excellent sources of support. Like members of Alcoholics Anonymous, participants in the Al-Anon family groups learn to work the Twelve Steps. They learn how destructive their attempts to control the uncontrollable are to themselves and others. Through the open sharing with other members they share experience, strength, and hope. They learn that *they* need and deserve help and begin their own personal recovery programs. Many of the lessons of Alanon apply to the psychiatric disorder as well. The concept of enabling, for example, is relevant to both groups. We like to supplement chemical dependency support groups with mental health support groups such as those run by the Alliance for the Mentally Ill. Parents and spouses of persons suffering from schizophrenia as well as other mental disorders share experiences and give support. Accepting that your loved one is mentally ill can be more difficult than accepting that he/she is an alcoholic. The stigma associated with mental illness can lead to guilt, fear, and feelings of loneliness for the family members of the mentally ill. A support group can be an excellent vehicle for learning acceptance and how to "detach with love" from the dually diagnosed family member.

Ideally, the family can attend both kinds of meetings. If this is difficult, we prefer to emphasize the chemical dependency support groups, since we feel these will address key issues applicable to both. We look forward to the day when there are dual diagnosis support groups for family members nationwide.

BEHAVIOR MANAGEMENT

The objective here is to provide a safe, stable, and reasonably flexible environment for family members to lay the foundation for further growth. The focus is on giving the family a set of rules for responding to situations involving such things as threats of harm to self or others, failure to take medication, the resumption of chemical use, disobedience, and the failure of the dually diagnosed family member to follow through on the ongoing recovery program. We introduce the dually disordered person into sessions at this time. Families benefit from the establishment of reasonable rules to moderate extremes of chaos or rigidity and to begin to establish appropriate boundaries.

We make great use of contracts in this endeavor and supplement them with behavioral rehearsal in which family members practice implementing the contract. Not only does the contract give a set of rules to govern family behavior, but the contract process gives families training in negotiating and problem-solving skills. Many families in early recovery tell us that the behavior contract was the only thing keeping the family sane in the early months of recovery. Appendix 4 presents a useful behavior contract for adolescents and their families developed by our colleagues, J. Douglas Myers, Ph.D., and George Howard, M.A. We use a variation of this contract with our adult clients.

SKILLS TRAINING

The objective of this intervention is to enhance family members' abilities to interact in a more functional manner. Families benefit from training and practice in such skills as assertion, communication, and negotiation and problem solving. Unlike the previous intervention with its emphasis on skillful behavior in targeted situations, the focus here is on higher-order skills applicable to a range of situations likely to be encountered in the future. With increased skills, family members can become their own "therapists" and respond to new situations in flexible and appropriate ways.

As the family settles into a firm early recovery, its members are ready to begin in-depth work focused on further growth. More traditional family therapy approaches are suitable here. Information about child developmental issues can also be helpful, as are specific tasks designed to strengthen appropriate spousal, parent–child, and sibling relationships. A key set of tasks focuses on a fundamental need in these families, the need for fun. Families caught up in reactive, unhealthy systems never had the time or energy to play together. Families need to move from a problem-centered to a growth-centered existence. Practicing play behaviors helps them do this and also assists in establishing a positive emotional atmosphere. In this stage family members can also learn to work through and resolve old hurts, resentments, and wounds and move on with their lives.

SPECIAL ISSUES

The sequence of interventions discussed above is ideal and assumes a family is willing and able to work on its recovery. Needless to say, the counselor or case manager often faces a less than ideal situation. In this section we discuss some specific common dilemmas that providers encounter with dual diagnosis families and share some of our solutions.

Sometimes the family of a dual diagnosis client has severed all connections. This is especially true for adults with a mental illness.

Sometimes a successful early recovery from both disorders sets the stage for a possible reunion, but this is not always the case. In these cases we focus on helping the client grieve the loss and move on with establishing a new life. At other times, the dual diagnosis client remains unmotivated for recovery despite our best efforts to break through denial and motivate him/her for change. We proceed by redefining our "client" as the family in these cases. At the very least family members can enter recovery. Ironically, this often prompts the client to start making positive changes.

Often the family feels that only the identified patient has a problem and that the service provider's job is to fix him or her. These families meet the suggestion that they need assistance with disbelief, anger, and resistance. Or, the identified patient is reluctant to have family members involved. In other cases an enabling spouse or parent "rescues" the client from treatment. Some providers and programs refuse to treat the client unless the family also participates, and this is certainly a viable option. We prefer to try several strategies that we and others have found useful (5,12,13). Counselors and case managers are more likely to obtain family cooperation if they:

1. Make the final determination on who needs to attend, using input from the identified patient but reserving the right of final decision.Contact the family as early as possible and communicate, kindly but firmly, the expectation they will participate.
2. Meet with the family as early as possible, ideally at the intake interview.
3. Call the sessions "consultations" or some other term that avoids a blaming and judgmental focus.
4. Accept the family's goals and explain how the session can help achieve this.
5. Have one therapist in charge of all contacts with both the identified patient and family whenever possible.
6. Position the therapists as experts with resources, and, whenever possible, do something useful for the family.
7. Use the family member with the power to get the other members into the sessions. Sometimes identified patients are very powerful, and joining with them or making something they want contingent on family participation is useful. If one parent is ambivalent, contact the other parent. If parent and child are strongly allied, have them work on other family members.

Chapters 9 and 10 contain further discussion of tactics that are effective for getting both the identified client and the family into treatment and keeping them there.

Often another family member is also chemically dependent or psychiatrically disordered (or both) and is unwilling to do anything about it. We handle this in a number of ways. Sometimes we make abstinence or psychiatric stability part of the home behavior contract and specify contingencies for a failure to maintain these behavioral objectives. Sometimes we orchestrate a family intervention as described in the next chapter, although we are hesitant to do this if the identified client is regressed or vulnerable to decompensation. We sometimes work toward getting all other interested family members into recovery, including the client, and help them practice loving detachment with the "nonidentified" client. In the case of an adolescent we use the term psychological emancipation to describe this process.

Sometimes the family situation poses an immediate health and safety risk. Families where there is violence and abuse fit this category. When this risk exists and relevant laws exist, we report child or senior abuse or facilitate court commitment for mandated treatment and let the established system run its course. With adults we will recommend separation and the use of such resources as battered women's shelters and restraining orders. In cases where a family member shows a potential for possible harm to others, we will help the family member develop contingency plans that specify his/her response to a dangerous situation. Examples include going to a relative or neighbor's house when the other family member is drunk or threatening. Often family members are more willing to change during a crisis, and counselors and case managers can use this opportunity to help the family begin to work toward more permanent solutions.

Families of the dual disordered client need counseling and support. Involving the family in counseling increases the chances of a positive treatment outcome.

REFERENCES

1. Beattie, M. Co-dependent No More. Harper/Hazelden, New York, 1987.
2. Barker, P. Basic Family Therapy. Oxford University Press, New York, 1986.
3. Alexander J., and Parsons, B. Short-term behavioral interventions with delinquents and their families. Journal of Abnormal Psychology, 81(4), 210–225, 1973.
4. Jacobsen, N. S., and Margolin, G. Marital Therapy: Strategies Based on Social Learning and Behavior Exchange Principles. Brunner/Mazel, New York, 1979.

5. Stanton, M. D., Todd, T. C., and Associates. *The Family Therapy of Drug Abuse and Addiction*. Guilford Press, New York, 1982.
6. Jacobsen, N. S. Family therapy outcome research: Potential pitfalls and prospects. *Journal of Marital and Family Therapy, 11*, 145–158, 1981.
7. Spencer, J. H., Glick, I. D., Hass, G. L., et al. A randomized trial of inpatient family intervention: III Effects at 6 month and 18 month follow-ups. *American Journal of Psychiatry, 145(9)*, 1115–1121, 1988.
8. Woitiz, J. G. *Adult Children of Alcoholics*. Health Communications, Pompano Beach, FL, 1983.
9. Black, C. *It Will Never Happen to Me*. M. A. C. Printing and Publications, Denver, 1982.
10. Leff, J. A. and Vaughn, C. *Expressed Emotion in Families*. Guilford Press, New York, 1985.
11. Steinglass, P. Family therapy with substance abuse other than alcohol. In T. B. Karasu (Ed.), *Treatments of Psychiatric Disorders*. American Psychiatric Association, Washington, D.C., pp. 1111–1117, 1989.
12. Epstein, N. B., and Bishop, D. S. Problem-centered systems therapy of the family. *Journal of Marital and Family Therapy, 7*, 23–31, 1981.
13. Szapoczink J., Perez-Vidal, A., Brickman, A. L., et al. Engaging adolescent drug abusers and their families in treatment: A strategic structural systems approach. *Journal of Consulting and Clinical Psychology, 56(4)*, 552–557, 1988.

9

Preventing Relapse and
Enhancing Motivation

Recovery from chemical dependency *or* a major psychiatric disorder is a long-term process with many possible pitfalls. Recovery from chemical dependency *and* a coexisting psychiatric disorder is even more of a challenge. The focus of this chapter is preventing relapse and promoting motivation for recovery with the dual diagnosis person.

THE PROBLEM

Mark Twain, an inveterate smoker of cigars, said it well: "Quitting smoking is easy, I've done it a thousand times." Stopping chemical use is probably less than half the battle. Staying stopped is the real struggle. How many next evening binges follow that morning's vow to quit? We worked with one person suffering from schizophrenia who was on a police hold for smashing a store's window. He told us after 3 days of an acute psychosis, "I don't know why I keep taking that speed, it always gets me into trouble."

We often poll participants in our workshops about their own change efforts. We first ask participants to raise their hands if they have attempted to change an important piece of behavior in the past year. Perhaps they decided to lose weight or spend more time with their kids. The majority raise their hands. We then ask all the people who did it right the first time and every time after that to keep their hands up. Generally all hands go down, although there is sometimes one

141

paragon of perfection. The point of this exercise is to remind providers how difficult change can be. We need to remember the struggle that dual diagnosis clients face when trying to change. By definition the dual diagnosis individual's problems have continued for some time and have caused him/her and his/her loved ones distress and disability. We cannot let the difficulty of change become an excuse. But we must have realistic expectations regarding outcomes and account for the difficulties of sustaining change in our treatment efforts.

Studies looking at various clinical populations suggest that relapse is a common problem. Studies vary, but estimates are that 50% to 90% of treated individuals with addictive behaviors relapse (1,2). Those with psychiatric disorders also relapse. As many as two-thirds of those people diagnosed with schizophrenia continue to have recurrences of their symptoms, and half of all people with major depression will have another episode (3).

An individual with both chemical dependency and major psychiatric disorder is likely to be at high risk for relapse. For both disorders the available research, however, is sparse. One study found that people diagnosed as having a borderline personality disorder while benefiting from chemical dependency treatment are at higher risk for relapse and continued difficulties than "standard" chemical dependency clients (4). A review of our own dual diagnosis patients concluded that most of them had a history of chronic relapses involving both drug and alcohol use as well as the symptoms of the mental disorder.

The failure of the client to remain both clean and sober and psychiatrically stable has several negative consequences. Clients, families, and providers can become pessimistic and burned out. Options can disappear as resources become exhausted. Clients and families often use up their insurance, and public sector providers sometimes refuse services in an attempt to conserve limited funding for cases more likely to respond. Finally, the client faces distress, disability, and even death.

We believe that preventing relapse must be a key focus of treatment with dual diagnosis clients and that this focus will decrease the chances of relapse.

THE RELAPSE PROCESS

Relapse is a medical term referring to the recurrence of the symptoms of a disease after improvement. Quite often providers and researchers have operationally defined relapse as a single event and used simple symptoms indexes to measure relapse. For the chemically dependent person, the indicator has been the use of any mood-altering chemicals. Either the person has used and has relapsed or has not used and has not relapsed. For the person with a psychiatric disorder, a common indicator has been the frequency of readmission to a psychiatric hospital (or in the case of a person with an antisocial personality, legal system involvement). Either the person has been rehospitalized or he/she has not. More sophisticated indicators of psychiatric relapse have included the return of hallucinations, lowered ratings of mood, or increased thoughts of self-harm.

Defining relapse as an "event" has the advantages of simplicity. But the "event" definition of relapse also has a number of problems. The single symptom approach to defining relapse focuses attention on the person in isolation from other factors and attributes relapse to causes internal to the client. The client might be referred to as unmotivated for change or as untreatable. Further treatment may be viewed as enabling or as not indicated for this client. The "event" approach also tends to focus attention on the acute symptoms of the problem, ignoring concomitant or associated difficulties.

Workers in the chemical dependency field or persons in A.A. are familiar with the terms "dry drunk" and "white knuckle sobriety." This refers to an individual who, although not actively drinking or using, maintains the attitudes and behaviors of a practicing alcoholic. Psychological rigidity and heightened moodiness are hallmarks of this syndrome and deserve treatment attention. Finally, the "event" approach tends to see the person as back to zero once relapsed. Clients and families, defining abstinence as the only goal, can react to use in a catastrophic black–white fashion, feeling that there's "no good in trying," and treatment didn't "work." They can feel that they might just as well stop trying to get better. This way of looking at relapses ignores the fact that often the client has made significant gains with treatment, such as staying out of the hospital for a whole year, or waking up the morning following a relapse with the absolute realization that "I am an addict! No more maybe about it!" Sometimes clients are labeled "retreads" and are placed into the exact treatment regimen prescribed prior to relapse, with little real work done on issues surrounding the relapse. The client experiences this "retreat for retreads" as a personal failure, adding to his/her decreased sense of self-worth.

Recent literature on relapse in addictive behaviors supports a view that relapse is a process and not an event (5,6). We prefer this view for dual diagnosis clients as well. This model has a number of elements when applied to persons with dual diagnosis. First, abstinence and psychiatric stability are the first, high priority objectives for the dual

diagnosis person but the long-term goal is recovery, defined as resolution of other associated difficulties and even enhancement of the
client's life. Second, recovery is a long-term, complex process ex-
tending over several years (and even a lifetime!) and must involve an
ongoing series of therapeutic experiences. Third, relapse most typically begins before the use of drugs or alcohol, and physiological,
psychological, and social factors play a role in this process. For
example, we have often seen an increase of thinking errors (e.g.,
blaming and rationalizing) several weeks or days prior to a relapse;
A.A. members refer to this same phenomenon with the phrase
"stinkin' thinkin.'" Fourth, the "relapse as a process" model makes
an important distinction between a lapse and a relapse (2). A lapse is a
recurrence of pretreatment behaviors, including an episode of chemical use, intensification of psychiatric symptoms, or both. Whether a
relapse then occurs depends on the client response to the lapse. The
continued use of old, ineffective solutions in response to a lapse is a
relapse, whereas use of new, healthier responses then constitutes only
a lapse. If individuals continue to work their program, they have not
necessarily relapsed. Conversely, if clients continue abstinent and
stable, they may not necessarily be "in recovery" if they are not
engaging in behavior likely to maintain abstinence and grow beyond it.
We use the term relapse mode to characterize this situation. The goal
then becomes helping the dual diagnosis person work a good recovery
program for both of his/her disorders, one likely first to prevent lapses
from becoming relapses and then likely to promote positive growth.
The dual diagnosis person may experience periodic crisis, but his/her
baseline functioning should be better each time.

An example may clarify these notions. We treated one person
diagnosed as schizophrenic with a 10-year history of heavy drinking
and failure to take her medications. Psychotic and drunk at admission,
she left treatment stable and sober. Three months later she presented
for admission after a 3-day alcohol bender. At readmission she stated
that she was "an alcoholic" and had relapsed and needed brief
inpatient care to get back on the right track. She looked physically fit
and spoke in a coherent fashion, because she had continued to take her
antipsychotic medication after leaving the hospital. After a short
inpatient stay that focused on fine-tuning her relapse prevention and
recovery plans, she returned to the community and has remained there
successfully for a year as of this writing. We would argue that this
client had experienced a lapse and not a relapse. She had used alcohol
but had responded to this use in new ways. She had immediately
sought help after her resumption of drinking and had continued to take
her medication. Was this a treatment success or failure? Time will tell,

but to date the client is recovering from both of her disorders and "working a program of recovery."

The "process" model of relapse has numerous strengths. The model promotes attention not only to abstinence but to other holistic issues. The inclusion of multiple variables such as the person's social environment increases the number of treatment options open to the provider. The client, family, and provider can also reframe any recurrence of symptoms as an opportunity for learning, fine-tuning, and progress and help avoid thinking in terms of failure or of malign client motives. Some research suggests that many persons make several change attempts before achieving success (7). And our own experience indicates that many of our clients have to experience relapses before "surrendering" and realizing that they have problems they must address. Hope is a better foundation for recovery than failure. This model can help providers and families hold clients accountable in a productive fashion. Blaming the person for having symptoms of a disease or disorder is not especially productive. Assisting people to be responsible for managing their disease or disorder is more helpful to them and the provider.

The "process" model of relapse also has a number of general implications for treating dual diagnosis clients. We believe strongly in a "continuum of care" for dual diagnosis clients. Because recovery is a long-term process and likely to involve backsliding, dual diagnosis persons need ongoing assistance and access to a variety of settings ranging from acute hospitalization to self-help groups to maintain gains and promote further progress. Providers working with chemically dependent clients have long emphasized the need for aftercare. This is doubly important for dual diagnosis clients. Suggesting to dual diagnosis clients that they go to 90 A.A. meetings in 90 days after 4 weeks of residential or inpatient care is helpful. Even more helpful is also teaching clients skills and providing additional structures to support continual recovery.

Continuum of care also relates to a second important implication of the "relapse as a process" model. Clients are at different stages of recovery and bring their own personal strengths and weaknesses to their recovery. Dual diagnosis individuals also bring the complications of their psychiatric disorder. We need to tailor recovery interventions not only to the stage of the recovery of dual diagnosis clients but also to their functional level. Sobriety and stability of the psychiatric disorder are the focus of early recovery. Again, the "outside-in" strategy discussed in Chapter 2 is a useful way to go about selecting an intervention. We begin structuring the external systems in the client's life. Everyone in early sobriety needs social support. Many persons suffering from chronic schizophrenia or other chronic disorders may always need social support, including placement in a residential setting where staff are familiar with chemical use issues. "First things first and start where the client is at" are useful maxims. Later interventions might include skills training and then perhaps more expressive, feelings-oriented therapy.

A third general guideline that we have found useful is to start relapse prevention work early in treatment. Once the dual diagnosis client commits to the need to manage his/her dual disorders (no matter how ambivalently) and is reasonably stable we begin helping him/her learn the distinction between lapses and relapses, plan ways to prevent relapse, and teach the skills necessary to do this. Waiting until aftercare can be counterproductive. What about that first pass outside the treatment center?

DETERMINANTS OF RELAPSE

Clinical experience and research have identified a number of factors increasing the risk of relapse (5). Knowing these factors allows the provider to determine the client's exposure in these areas and to select high priority interventions. The A.A. community uses the acronym *HALTS* to specify conditions increasing the risk of relapse. Recovering alcoholics who are *hungry, angry, lonely, tired,* or *sick* are more likely to relapse. Research on addictive behaviors and psychiatric disorders has identified a number of such variables that can contribute to relapse.

Biological Factors

Genetic factors appear to play a role in the way individuals metabolize chemicals. *High tolerance levels* suggest an individual primed for uncomfortable withdrawal symptoms. A *poor response to neuroleptic medication* indicates a client with chronic psychiatric symptoms. Recent research has implicated processes such as *Pavlovian conditioning effects* in relapse, especially with cocaine and crack (8). Mere exposure to cues historically associated with use or withdrawal can apparently trigger cravings and withdrawal symptoms. An *extroverted temperament* with a propensity for sensation-seeking activity can make renewed use a temptation (9). Many antisocial individuals exhibit such a temperament. The manic client who's known for highly impulsive behavior is also relapse prone. *Physiological states* similar to withdrawal states can trigger relapse, hence the relevance of the HALTS acronym cited earlier.

Psychological Variables

The best predictor of relapse for addictive behaviors and a number of psychiatric disorders is the experience of *negative emotional states* (3,5,10). Almost universally, high rates of stressful life events, especially so-called social exits (e.g., deaths, divorces, end of a significant relationship), lead to increased relapse rates for all disorders. Getting angry, depressed, or anxious primes relapse behavior. Continued *positive expectations* of use is another psychological factor related to relapse (2,10). How many of us have had clients say they only had fun when high, romanticizing their use, and forgetting all the negative consequences of their use? Failure to learn how to "have fun" in sobriety exacerbates this problem. *Increasing use of thinking errors* or other patterns of distorted thinking (6) is also a factor in relapse. Excuse making, victimizing, or engaging in "I'm unique" thinking provides a ready-made way to justify backing out of a recovery program. Finally, an *impoverished life style* is an important factor, especially for dual diagnosis clients (5). If all they have is their use and their disorder, why recover? Sitting around alone in an apartment for hours, thinking about not using, with nothing to look forward to is a setup for all kinds of problems.

Social Factors

Poor social support is associated with relapse for both chemical dependency and psychiatric disorders (2,3). Research studies have clearly demonstrated that persons with an impoverished social support system are at higher risk for depression, for example. Family, friends, and self-help groups provide emotional and material resources promoting recovery. *Peer pressure* and *interpersonal conflict* are also risk factors for relapse (2,5). Fighting, arguments, and unreasonable demands for behavior cause those suffering from schizophrenia, even when on medications, to become psychotic (3). Friends say "just have one." The family of the dual diagnosis client, as the focal point of many of these social processes, is a key element in promoting (or hindering) recovery and family work has to be a high priority as discussed in Chapter 8.

SOME TECHNIQUES

We have found a number of interventions useful in preventing relapse during the early stages of recovery. Generally we teach basic principles of relapse prevention in a group/class format and then work individually with clients to apply these principles to their own specific situation. This last part is important because this allows us to check the client's comprehension and to assist the client (many of whom have difficulty translating ideas into action because of the psychiatric disorder) to apply these principles to his/her own unique situation.

Attendance at A.A., N. A., Al-Anon, and similar meetings is crucial and the available data suggest this is effective (11,12), at least for persons with one disorder. "Ninety meetings in 90 days" is a common prescription for chemically dependent persons and also serves dual diagnosis people well when combined with other interventions. We introduce our hospitalized clients to A.A. type procedures in "mock" meetings as soon as possible to help them become familiar and comfortable with the structure of Twelve Step meetings. As soon as they can tolerate it, we have our clients attend meetings offered in the hospital and then transition them to meetings in the local community. We try to identify meetings that are tolerant of, and even supportive of, the behaviors and special needs of dual diagnosis people. Where such meetings do not already exist, some providers have started dual-diagnosis-sympathetic community meetings or, especially with seriously dysfunctional clients in smaller, more traditional communities, offer special meetings at their treatment centers. A recovering staff member familiar with mental health issues is an invaluable resource for initiating these groups and, with time, the clients provide increasing amounts of leadership.

We like to supplement Twelve Step self-help meetings with additional *support groups* such as Recovery, Inc. For the more regressed client, medication groups to monitor and enhance compliance with medication or day treatment programs to support the higher functioning client are useful. We try to help clients identify family or friends whom they can turn to for support, and we assist them to increase the number of such individuals available to them. A treatment plan objective that we commonly specify is to have the client identify three sources of support and practice using one of them in the coming week.

"Birds of a feather flock together" goes the saying, and dual diagnosis clients often have old friends who use chemicals. Many of these clients also have trouble making new friends. Chronically mentally ill individuals often live in single room occupancy hotels characterized by chaos, crime, and chemicals. These are places unlikely to promote stability and sobriety and suitable housing is important. Many adolescents with dual disorders are members of gangs or other groups likely to support antisocial behavior and chemical use.

The task facing the dual diagnosis person is the development of *prorecovery peer groups*. In our experience, clients find this very difficult. Those with using "friends" find disengagement very difficult and need assistance in locating and cultivating positive peers. Many clients will also need to grieve the loss of their old, using peer group as well.

Although many adult dual diagnosis clients no longer have involved families, many do, and *family work* is crucial. Families are a key ingredient in relapse prevention and need to be included in relapse prevention planning.

We also use other kinds of interventions to decrease the likelihood of relapse. We make great use of *contracts* to clarify expectations, provide structure, and enhance motivation. These contracts specify that the client (and family in many cases) have the goals of sobriety and stability for the reasons stated on the contract and agree to follow these rules and make use of these resources to achieve these goals. These contracts typically include a penalty clause for failure to live up to the terms of the agreement and, in some instances, rewards for compliance. The ritual of making contracts often seems to carry great weight with clients and provides a structure for providers as well. Review and revision of contracts makes a great task for weekly treatment sessions.

Planning for relapse prevention is crucial. We don't shy away from bringing up the possibility of relapse with clients. Just as with suicide, talking to the client about relapse will not make it happen. Indeed, our experience is that many dual diagnosis clients already have a secret relapse scenario in their heads, and research has demonstrated that client self-ratings of likelihood of success predict future outcome very well (5). Raising the issue of relapse is a good way to puncture unrealistic, overly optimistic, "pink cloud" thinking and to desensitize the client to the prospect of future difficulties. Many people who have demonstrated an ability to joke and laugh respond well to a "Devil's advocate" stance. The provider can gently challenge the client's "I'm all fixed" notions and probe for relapse scenarios. For more concrete, rigid, or controlling clients we often use a fire drill metaphor. Just as fires seldom happen but require fire drills "just-in-case," we frame relapse work as also "just-in-case" something were to happen.

We make frequent use of a process that we call *failsafing*. We do failsafe planning for each problem on the person's treatment plan. We work with the individual and significant others to identify triggers that have historically, or are likely in the future, to set off a relapse. We then ask the client first to write down the triggers and then to write behaviors likely to short circuit the relapse. We ask clients to write these on index cards that they can carry in their pocket or purse. One person diagnosed with schizophrenia called them his "therapist-in-a-pocket." Examples of triggers include things such as "thinking I don't need this medication," "an argument with my wife," or "being alone." Examples of helpful behaviors include such things as calling the crisis hotline (with phone number listed on the card), going to an A.A. meeting, or using assertive statements. The more specific to the person's situation and level of functioning, the more helpful are the failsafe cards.

Both clients and providers enjoy the failsafe process. It establishes a collaborative relationship, generates great assessment data, and teaches problem solving. The failsafe process provides a wonderful focus for sessions in early recovery and results in a tangible, rewarding counseling product. Many clients become very involved in the failsafe process. Some have called us saying that they are experiencing many triggers and need additional help. Individuals readmitted to our program sometimes indicate that their first task is to redesign their failsafe cards because "calling mother" made things worse. In keeping with our lapse/relapse distinction, we see this as tremendous progress.

The provider and client can set up ongoing *monitoring processes*. A standard one is random urine drug screening. This not only detects relapse but helps keep the client honest by providing external controls and support. We also encourage clients and sometimes families to monitor possible antecedents to relapse such as an increase in thinking errors, signs of impending depression or psychosis (such as isolation and withdrawal), or the failure to attend support group meetings. Journals, checklists of triggers, or thinking error inventories done on a daily or weekly basis help prevent relapse. These monitoring activities keep sobriety and stability salient for everyone involved and provide motivation for keeping on task. These activities also promote honesty, the antidote to denial and a fundamental requirement for recovery.

Providers and, where pertinent, families also need *relapse protocols* that have explicit policies and procedures that detail the response to a client relapse. We do not terminate services or administratively discharge a client in treatment from care with a documented relapse. We are concerned that this places too much blame on the client. We prefer instead to adopt a relapse "loop" process. We will supply a negative consequence such as loss of privileges but permit the client to earn back these privileges after completing a series of special relapse exercises. Our own exercises ask the client to write out (or audiotape) his/her responses to these questions: (1) What triggered your relapse? (2) What happened when you relapsed? (3) How did you fail to be responsible for your own behavior? (4) What could you have done differently? (5) What will you do differently next time? (6) Why do you think you should forgive yourself for relapsing? (7) How do you plan to avoid future relapses? When the person has completed this assignment to the satisfaction of the provider, the client then has the opportunity to earn back his/her previous privileges in our status system. Depending on the nature of the relapse (use of chemicals, cutting self, skipping school), we also ask clients to read relevant material and to write an essay on the application of the readings to the prevention of a future relapse. We have used similar approaches for outpatients, assigning patients to special relapse "sessions" or groups and having them work on similar assignments. We feel that this procedure holds clients accountable while supporting their efforts to change.

One of the challenges of maintaining sobriety is to overcome the positive rewards of relapse behavior. The "quick fix" yields immediate rewards, whereas the negative consequences of use are more often long-term. Conversely, staying sober and stable is difficult and the most positive rewards are often experienced over the long term. In addition, human beings universally tend to remember the good times in the past and to focus on the tough times coming ahead. *Expectation exercises* are useful for dealing with these psychological processes. The A.A. ritual of telling your story and the A.A. slogans of "one day at a time" and "this too shall pass" are useful remedies for dealing with these psychological realities. We also like to work with clients to enable them to tell their stories with an emphasis on how bad things were, what happened, and how much better things are now with recovery. Individuals also write out lists of short-term and long-term positive and negative consequences associated with their use and with their psychiatric disorder (2). We also ask them to list the costs and benefits of sobriety and stability. Discussion of these lists helps to keep clients oriented to the reality of their situation. If appropriate, we do similar exercises using visual imagery to recall the past and imagine the future, encouraging clients to recall the negatives of their dual disorders when these are active and the benefits of recovery. We also discourage the telling of war stories and the glamorizing of use.

As the client advances in recovery or shows higher functional levels we make *skills training* a focus (2). Given the enormous impact of negative emotional states, we like to focus on helping clients develop better ways to handle anxiety, anger, and depression. Training in relaxation techniques, assertiveness, problem-solving skills, and constructive thinking equip clients better to avoid negative emotional states and to cope with them when they do occur. We might teach less functional clients to take times out, start a conversation, or do crafts activities to help them manage similar affects.

More globally, we also like to assist the client to achieve a more *balanced life style* (2), with appropriate amounts of work, play, and love. Sitting around in your apartment thinking "I must not drink or cut myself" is no way to prevent relapse and promote a well-balanced program of recovery.

Dual diagnosis people often have few positives in their lives other than their use. We employ weekly scheduling to promote a more balanced lifestyle. Using a Sunday through Saturday, 6:00 a.m. to midnight, hour by hour sheet, we ask clients to write in their current weekly activities. We discuss gaps and imbalances and ask the client to do an improved schedule. The next session we review what happened and problem-solve around failures. Many clients achieve a more balanced life style using this approach.

Stress and chemical use, together with haphazard attention to regular meals and disruption of sleep patterns, typically leave dual diagnosis individuals physiologically depleted. *Nutritional counseling* as well as attention to regular *self-care routines* are helpful in preventing relapse and promoting recovery. A marvelous remedy is exercise (5). Besides providing a positive "addiction" and supplying natural biochemical mood enhancers and stress modifiers, the attainment of fitness enhances the client's sense of personal competence and worth. Consultation with appropriate medical authorities is important here, especially for the older client who should probably not start marathon running without a check-up and, instead, should enjoy the success of walking daily for several months. Many providers report that vitamins and nutritional supplements are helpful.

We like to develop a written *recovery plan* for each client early in treatment. We always include attendance at Twelve Step meetings and failsafe work in the plan but will often emphasize a selection of the strategies outlined above. The client's personal risk factors, functional level, and stage of recovery guide our selection. Too many interventions will overwhelm the client (and the provider!). Better to do two things well than seven things poorly. You can always renegotiate the recovery plan over time.

No clear guidelines exist to help determine whether the dual diagnosis client has transitioned from early recovery (with the emphasis on sobriety and stability) to later recovery (with the emphasis on resolution and enhancement) (13). Relapse and recovery always remain issues but the emphasis shifts with time and patient progress. Research suggests that the great majority of chemically dependent individuals who relapse will relapse in the first 3 months (1) but that there is no totally "safe" point (5). Given the variety of outcomes for different psychiatric disorders, no all-purpose safe point is likely and assessment of each individual is necessary. One year is the bench mark used by many clinicians and, in the absence of data, seems sufficient to provide a general guideline for evaluating progress. Consequently, dual diagnosis persons must work a program to prevent relapse but the emphasis can generally shift after the first year to focus more on long-term recovery issues depending on the progress a given individual has made and his/her compliance with working a program. Continued involvement in Twelve Step recovery self-help groups and focus on "working the steps" on a daily basis will promote long-term recovery. Often, more traditional therapies are also useful for helping people deal with other issues as they arise.

Life continues for the recovering dual diagnosis client, and sobriety and stability are not guarantees of total happiness and a life free of conflict and problems. We worked with one client, a person suffering from schizophrenia, with a 10-year history of alcohol abuse and psychosis prior to dual diagnosis treatment. He called our admissions staff in a panic on a Saturday after his discharge from our hospital. His beloved grandmother had died the night before and he was upset and made vague complaints of suicidal thinking. However, he had maintained 18 months of sobriety and stability, was attending A.A., and was working with a therapist from the local mental health center. Rather than rehospitalize him, we validated his feelings of grief, helped him identify his support systems in A.A. and at the mental health program, and set up a twice a day phone check-in procedure through the weekend. With his permission, we also contacted his case manager at the mental health clinic on Monday. This particular person did just fine with some additional support in a time of personal crisis. Dual diagnosis individuals will always need a little extra. We have found that by providing the extra care in the beginning, long-term success with this population is more likely.

THE MOTIVATION ISSUE

A crucial issue in the treatment of not only single diagnosis but also dual diagnosis persons is the matter of motivation. Providers and others experience difficulty when attempting to get many dually diagnosed persons to commit to treatment and to maintain this commitment. Another related issue is whether dual diagnosis clients are genuinely committed to treatment or whether they are merely faking it because of external pressures, and hence, are likely to fail in treatment. This is especially true for persons with a coexisting personality disorder.

The denial and deficits associated with chemical abuse and psychiatric disorders can often make dually diagnosed persons unwilling and/or unable to engage consistently in treatment. However, seeing the focus of the problem as residing solely in the person and attempting to judge whether the person "really" means it has some difficulties. Research has demonstrated that expecting client noncompliance can actually increase its probability, and this mind set can discourage providers (and families) from attempting to influence the dually diagnosed person's therapeutic compliance in a positive fashion (14). We have also found that staff discussions of whether the dually diagnosed person is genuinely committed can be a trap and can ignore the complexity of change and the ambivalence associated with change.

As discussed in the next chapter in greater detail, we certainly do not advocate unreasonable efforts to manage the unmanageable. However, we have found it more useful to focus on behavioral compliance as one measure of treatment success and to believe the well-established psychological principle that attitude change often follows behavior change. We have also found it useful to adopt some of the techniques from the treatment compliance literature (see Ref. 15) in helping dually diagnosed clients enter and remain in treatment.

Having external *levers* such as court orders, keeping a job, obtaining financial resources, or a spouse with a bag packed and ready to leave can sometimes be useful for getting clients into treatment. Reminding them of these pending consequences during treatment can also help to maintain compliance. One objection to this maneuver is that, as soon as the pressure is off, the compliance will cease. Research has demonstrated that such measures can increase compliance and that outcomes at least for chemically dependent individuals are similar to those for voluntary ones (14,16). We have treated a number of "involuntary" voluntary dually diagnosed individuals and have found that treatment, especially when making the resistance the focus, often dissolves the resistance.

An *intervention* is another way to motivate clients. Experts in the field of chemical dependency are familiar with this process (see Ref. 17). In this process the alcoholic's significant others close to the person present the facts about the emotional impact on them of the alcoholic's behavior. The significant others give these data in a "we love you and care about you" style and not in an angry, blaming manner. This "moment of truth" often breaks through the denial and results in entry into treatment. We have seen these techniques adapted for use with dual diagnosis individuals including those with a coexisting bipolar disorder or anorexia.

The general principle with interventions is that expanding the social system can provide sources of motivation. We have had a great deal of success with mobilizing family, friends, other providers, program staff, and even prorecovery peers to talk with a client who is balking at entering or staying in treatment.

Interventions can be a high-risk, high-gain strategy, especially with dual diagnosis clients. By raising the "bottom" that the addict or psychiatric client has to hit to "surrender," clients and their families can avoid the progression of the disease and enter recovery before things get even more out of hand. On the other hand, interventions can go quite badly, resulting in severe, permanent damage to the relationships among clients and their significant others. Clients can refuse to go into or remain in treatment. Family members can blame each other for this failure. Intervention can even provoke violence when families attempt an intervention with a volatile dual diagnosis client such as an individual with a paranoid schizophrenic disorder. Intervention with dual diagnosis clients requires an understanding of the interaction of the two disorders and careful preparation to avoid a disaster.

Prior to planning any intervention, always consult with a trained expert. In the case of a dual diagnosis client, be sure to have a diagnosis of what the client's coexisting disorder is likely to be. Also use an interventionist familiar with both chemical dependency and mental health issues.

Sometimes a gentler approach is effective for motivating dual diagnosis clients to change. *Discussions of the negative consequences* of their chemical use and/or failure to deal with their psychiatric disorder can set the groundwork for entry into treatment. Remember that repetition is important for many dual diagnosis persons to learn. This includes real-life repeated experience of these negative consequences as well as ongoing discussions of these experiences. The provider can do this in one-to-one sessions or in groups. Examination of negative consequences in a matter-of-fact style and without condemnation can create a "safe" atmosphere that can disarm the fight/flight response and decrease denial (13). *Pointing out thinking errors* can also be helpful.

Tapping the client's goals is also useful for motivating him/her. We work hard to understand the concerns of the client and try to use these concerns to formulate a mutually acceptable goal. For example, some dual diagnosis people do not want treatment for their disorders. But these same people are quite willing to work with us on staying out of the hospital or getting their spouse "off their back." We can often share these goals and serve as a resource to help the client to achieve these goals. Frequently *emphasizing our joint* goals helps to keep the client on track, and us out of power struggles, and it enhances our credibility as "helpers" with the client.

A *smooth referral* from one care provider to the next increases the likelihood the person will stay engaged in the continuum of care. In our experience clients are more likely to follow through with the treatment plan if they have a chance to meet their next provider and visit a site prior to entry into that system. Having an appointment for admission or session already set is also helpful. Phone calls or notes between providers indicating that clients are arriving and returning as planned help with compliance. This can alert providers to the start of trouble and can provide support for clients who know that their care "committee" is monitoring the situation, tracking their progress, and serving as a strong support system.

We use *treatment contracts* extensively. These include basic expectations contracts wherein dually diagnosed clients acknowledge their informed consent to the basic goals of treatment and policies and procedures governing issues such as confidentiality, attendance, and relapse while in treatment. We also negotiate a treatment contract or service plan with the individual and/or family. We even start each session with a verbal minicontract regarding the purpose of this particular meeting. Contracts appear to enhance client compliance in a number of ways, including the establishment of clear expectations, the provision of choice for clients, and the setting of goals (see Ref. 14). Contracts also provide a set of guidelines for keeping treatment on track and measuring progress. Many clients with flagging motivation respond to reminders about the contract and to the success represented by achieving objectives of the plan.

Contracts are more likely to be effective if they are specific, time-limited, achievable, as well as if they state expectations in terms of what the parties will do (and not what they will not do) and specify consequences (see Ref. 18). Conversely, we have encountered several frequent pitfalls in negotiating contracts with dual diagnosis clients. These include language that is vague, specifying consequences the provider cannot control, and not having access to data regarding client compliance. Other pitfalls include making exceptions to the terms of the contract without explicitly renegotiating the terms and failing to get clients to agree explicitly and specifically to the terms of the contract.

Additional techniques we have used include having the client hang in there "just one more day" and urging clients to take "one day at a time"; discussing the long-term rewards of recovery and the consequences of various decisions; and, most importantly, engaging the client in a supportive (but not enabling) relationship from the start.

Despite our best efforts, however, some dual diagnosis clients refuse to enter treatment or leave services prematurely. In these cases we sometimes proceed to redefine the client, preferring to work instead with the significant others who are often trying to cope with both the identified client and their own difficulties. We proceed by giving them information and referring them to support groups such as Al-Anon. Engaging significant others in their own treatment is helpful to them and, ironically, sometimes results in the original client reengaging in treatment. And at other times we just have to accept that we have done the best we can do.

REFERENCES

1. Hunt, W. A., Barnett, L. W., and Branch, L. G. Relapse rates in addiction programs. *Journal of Clinical Psychology, 27,* 455–456, 1971.
2. Marlatt, G. A., and Gordon, J. K. (Eds.). *Relapse Prevention: Maintenance Strategies in the Treatment of Addictive Behaviors.* Guilford Press, New York, 1985.
3. Leff, J. P., and Vaughn, C. *Expressed Emotion in Families.* Guilford Press, New York, 1985.
4. Nace, E. P., Saxon, J. J., and Shore, N. Borderline personality disorder and alcoholism treatment: A one year follow-up study. *Journal of Studies on Alcoholism, 47,* 196–200, 1986.
5. Brownell, K. D., Marlatt, G. A., Lichtenstein, E., and Wilson, G. T. Understanding and preventing relapse. *American Psychologist, 7,* 765–782, 1986.
6. Gorski, T. T. *Passages through Recovery: An Action Plan for Preventing Relapse.* Harper & Row, New York, 1989.
7. Schacter, S. Recidivism and self-cure of smoking and obesity. *American Psychologist, 37,* 436–444, 1982.
8. Niaura, R. S., Rohsenow, D. J., Binkoff, J. A., et al. Relevance of cue reactivity to understanding alcohol and smoking relapse. *Journal of Abnormal Psychology, 97(2),* 133–152, 1988.
9. Nace, E. Alcoholism and other psychiatric disorders. In *The Treatment of Alcoholism.* Brunner/Mazel, New York, 1987.
10. Cooper, M. C., Russell, M., and George, W. H. Coping, expectancies and alcohol abuse: A test of social learning formulations. *Journal of Abnormal Psychology, 7(2),* 218–230, 1988.
11. Gartner, A., and Reissman, M. (Eds.). *The Self-Help Revolution.* Human Sciences Press, New York, 1984.
12. Galanter, M. Zealous self-help groups as adjuncts to psychiatric treatment:

A study of Recovery, Inc. *American Journal of Psychiatry, 145(10),* 1248–1253, 1988.

13. Brown, S. *Treating the Alcoholic: A Developmental Model of Recovery.* John Wiley & Sons, New York, 1985.

14. Miller, W. Motivation for treatment: A review with a special emphasis on alcoholism. *Psychiatric Bulletin, 48(1),* 84–107, 1985.

15. Meichenbaum, D., and Turk, D. C. *Facilitating Treatment Adherence: A Practioner's Guidebook.* Plenum Press, New York, 1987.

16. Watson, C. G., Brown, K., Tilleskjor, C., et al. The comparative recidivism rates of voluntary and coerced-admission male alcoholics. *Journal of Clinical Psychology, 44(4),* 573–581, 1988.

17. Picard, F. *Family Intervention: Ending the Cycle of Addiction and Codependency.* Beyond Words Publishing, Hillsboro, OR, 1989.

18. DeRisi, W. J., and Batz, G. *Writing Behavioral Contracts: A Case Simulation Practice Manual.* Research Press, Champaign, IL, 1975.

10

Case Management Strategies

Counseling and case managing dual diagnosis clients can be demanding and challenging. This chapter discusses some of the factors that, in our experience, make this task so difficult. The chapter also presents some suggestions for making the provider's job more manageable.

THE TRIANGLE

Counselors and case managers will find it helpful to be alert to possible dysfunctional dynamics in their helping relationships with dual diagnosis individuals. The Karpman triangle (cited in Ref. 1) suggests that a triangle with three roles succinctly summarized many of the relationships that clients often had with significant others. The triangle looks like this:

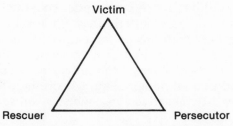

The triangle has three points corresponding to three different but complementary roles. These roles are those of victim, rescuer, and persecutor. Two individuals in a dysfunctional transaction take two complementary roles on the triangle. Although most individuals "on the triangle'' have preferred roles, very commonly the individuals switch roles on the triangle as they continue to interact. Sometimes a third person, a family, or another agency is on the triangle but for the sake of simplicity the focus here is on two individuals.

Counseling and case managing are also relationships and the Karpman triangle can help us understand the dynamic dilemmas that counselors and case managers experience with some of their dual diagnosis clients. Many clients enter a helping relationship as victims, feeling helpless, overwhelmed, and without control or responsibility for the situation. They look for someone else to "fix" the situation. Counselors and case managers can take on the rescuer role in response. Providers in the rescue mode assume all responsibility for the client's progress, attempt to make the client do what's good for him or her, and protect clients from the negative consequences of their actions. If progress fails to materialize, either the client or helper can then switch to the persecutor role. The persecutor does not focus on specific negative behaviors but blames the other person in general for any failures to achieve positive change. The persecutor attempts to coerce the other person to change by the use of criticism and other negative consequences and often ends up angry, blaming, and frustrated. These three complementary stances tend to elicit each other in systematic ways and any client and provider caught on the triangle typically go around and around in the triangular struggle. Some clients can strongly pull for a complementary role from the counselor or case manager. This is especially true of clients with strong denial or with personality disorders, who by definition have dysfunctional interpersonal relationships with others and who have had years of "practice" with such relationships. Helpers, by personality, training, or professional/organizational norms, can be vulnerable to the client's pull for a linked role on the triangle.

The goal for counselors or case managers is to stay off the triangle. They can be helpful but not rescuing, offer constructive feedback and limit setting but not persecution; they understand the differences between having legitimate needs for help and support and being a victim. Helpers will work best if they believe that the client is ultimately responsible for change, the counselor can ultimately control only herself, and that, although change is difficult for the client, the experience of realistic negative consequences can sometimes actually facilitate client change.

STRATEGIES

We have found several specific strategies useful for helping us stay off the triangle. Maintaining a *"doing business" stance* is important. We strive to avoid supporting clients' world views of being "victims" of other providers or agencies, "persecuting" clients because they are bad (instead of ill), or "rescuing" clients by making exceptions to contracts, policies, and procedures so as to avoid giving honest feedback and real consequences. Our job is to assist clients to take responsibility for themselves and to provide them, to the best of our ability, with the resources and tools so that they can do this.

We like to focus on *specifics*. Too often vague, global, or abstract discussion of a client's complaints, fears, and even satisfactions paves the way for triangular dynamics. Problem solving requires data, and keeping to the data helps to prevent issues other than the relevant issue from becoming a focus of the session. Statements such as "You're a bad therapist" or "That will never work" can lose their power to elicit the Karpman roles when followed by questions such as "Bad in what way?" or "How, specifically, will that not work?"

Maintaining *structure* in our contacts has been productive. Dual diagnosis clients can have difficulty remaining organized and maintaining boundaries. Developing and following policies and procedures helps. This is especially important for such issues as the management of high risk acting out behavior such as assault or self-harm, noncompliance with treatment, and even ways to change the policies and procedure or get an exception. Frequent or long staff conferences or client complaints of inconsistent treatment can all be indications of a problem in this area. Within reason, the exact nature of the policies and procedures does not matter. What does matter is that they be consistent with the philosophy of treatment, the treatment session, and the capabilities and resources of the office or agency. As discussed in Chapter 9, contracts are another excellent way to maintain structure.

Emphasizing positives has a number of advantages. Change is difficult and clients need reminders of their strengths, past successes, and the likelihood of future positive experiences. We have also found this an effective antidote for negative feelings we might have toward a client. Many annoying or frustrating behaviors actually have a positive intent or can be strengths in certain situations. Reframing these behaviors in this way for both ourselves and the persons we are treating has helped us stay off the triangle. For example, arguing the terms of a contract might be resistance or might indicate a concern for appropriate treatment on the part of the client.

Clear communication is important. We like to check out what the client heard us say by asking questions and asking the client to repeat back to us what we did say. Some dual diagnosis clients may not understand us or may misinterpret us more often than we sometimes suspect. Checking and rechecking helps us insure that our messages got through the way we intended. We also make an effort voluntarily to paraphrase and summarize client communications.

When it appears the client is engaging in a endless arguments, a good strategy is to *make a process comment* and get out of the content of the discussion. The thinking errors material discussed in Chapter 3 provides a useful set of words for commenting on process. We also like to teach our clients about the Karpman triangle, and this provides both parties with a set of terms for describing these dynamics.

We find it important to *coordinate with others*. Dual diagnosis clients often have multiple providers, and reconciling all the various goals, opinions, and points of view is necessary to help both the client and us stay off the triangle. Having frequent staffings or phone contacts keeps things clear, organized, and consistent. Designating a primary case manager whenever possible or clearly specifying areas of responsibility assists all parties in maintaining good working relationships. This can prevent care givers from different agencies from getting pulled into the Karpman triangle.

However accomplished, staying "off the triangle" will help you and your client deal with a difficult situation.

REFERENCE

1. Steiner, C. M. *Scripts People Live*. Grove Press, New York, 1974.

APPENDIXES

Appendix 1: Modified Stepwork

MODIFIED FOR THE SCHIZOPHRENIC CLIENT AND ORGANIC MENTAL DISORDERS

STEP 1

"We admitted we were powerless over alcohol [and drugs]—that our lives have become unmanageable."

PART 1

Give two examples of problems you now have that are related to your drinking and using.

PART 2

Give two examples of trouble you have gotten into because of your drinking and using.

PART 3

Please check the following which you feel apply to you:
- ☐ People tell me I drink or use too much.
- ☐ Others get mad at me when I drink or use.
- ☐ I've tried to stop drinking/using before but started up again.
- ☐ Sometimes I drink or use more than I planned

STEP 2

"Came to believe that a power greater than ourselves can restore us to sanity."

PART 1

Give one example of how things are getting better since you stopped drinking or using.

PART 2

Give one example of someone who has been of help to you and explain why.

PART 3

Please check those of the following that applied to you when you were drinking or using drugs:
- ☐ I lied to my friends or family.
- ☐ I stole or took things that didn't belong to me.
- ☐ I had fights or arguments with people.
- ☐ Friends or family didn't want me around them when I was drinking or using drugs.

STEP 3

"We turned our wills and lives over to the care of God as we understand Him."

PART 1

Give one example of something that you now worry about.

PART 2

Give an example of a person who you think is helpful to you or you could trust at least a little.

PART 3

How can it help you to "turn it over" or discuss this worry with the person you trust?

MODIFIED FOR THE MANIC–DEPRESSIVE CLIENT

STEP 1

"We admitted we were powerless over alcohol [and drugs]—that our lives have become unmanageable."

PART 1

List three examples (no more than 100 words each) of how you have gotten into trouble because of drinking and using.

PART 2

Give two examples of "rules" you have about drinking or using, which you developed in order to try to control your drinking or your use of drugs (not to exceed 25 words each).

PART 3

Give one example of how you have had to modify, change, or break the rules in Part 2 in order to continue to drink or use (no more than 25 words each).

STEP 2

"Came to believe a power greater than ourselves could restore us to sanity."

PART 1

Check those of the following mistakes in thinking or thinking errors that you can identify in yourself in relationship to your drinking or using:
- ☐ Excuse making
- ☐ Blaming
- ☐ Justifying
- ☐ Superoptimism
- ☐ Lying
- ☐ Threatening others
- ☐ Presenting false image
- ☐ Building up self

☐ Assuming
☐ "I'm unique"
☐ Grandiose thinking
☐ Intellectualizing
☐ Hostile and angry outbursts
☐ Making fools of others
☐ Playing victim
☐ Exaggeration
☐ Redefining
☐ Minimizing
☐ Ingratiating

PART 2

Give two examples of how your drinking and/or drug use were "insane" (no more than 50 words each).

PART 3

Give two examples of how your life has improved since you stopped drinking or using drugs.

STEP 3

"We made a decision to turn our will and lives over to the care of God as we understand Him."

PART 1

Give two brief examples (no more than 50 words each) of how you have tried to control your behavior and failed.

PART 2

Give two brief examples (no more than 50 words each) of situations where you tried to control someone else's behavior and failed.

PART 3

Give two examples of people who have been or could be helpful to you (no more than 25 words each).

PART 4

Give two examples of current problems you are having and describe how "turning it over" or talking with a helpful or trusted person would strengthen your recovery and reduce your anxiety (no more than 100 words each).

MODIFIED FOR THE BORDERLINE CLIENT

STEP 1

"We admitted we were powerless over alcohol [and drugs]—that our lives have become unmanageable."

PART 1

Describe five situations where you suffered negative consequences as a result of drinking or using drugs.

PART 2

List at least five "rules" you have about drinking or using drugs (example: I never drink alone).

PART 3

Give one example for each rule discussed in Part 2 of where and how you broke that rule.

PART 4

Check those of the following that apply to you:

- ☐ I sometimes drink or use more than I planned.
- ☐ I sometimes lie about my drinking or using.
- ☐ I have hidden or stashed away drugs or alcohol so I could use them alone or at a later time.
- ☐ I have had memory loss when drinking or using.
- ☐ I have tried to hurt myself when drinking or using.
- ☐ I can drink more than I used to, without feeling drunk.
- ☐ My personality changes when I drink or use.
- ☐ I have school or work problems related to my drinking or using.
- ☐ I have family problems related to my drinking or using.
- ☐ I have legal problems related to my drinking or using.

PART 5

Give two examples for each item checked in Part 4.

STEP 2

"We came to believe that a power greater than ourselves could restore us to sanity."

PART 1

Give three examples of how your drinking or using was insane (remember one definition of insanity is to keep repeating the same mistake and expecting a different outcome).

PART 2

Check which of the mistakes or thinking errors you use, then explain how this is harmful to yourself and others:

☐ Blaming
☐ Lying
☐ Manipulating
☐ Excuse making
☐ Minimizing
☐ Thinking I'm unique
☐ Cutting oneself when angry
☐ Negative self-talk
☐ Intellectualizing
☐ Using angry behavior to control others
☐ Beating yourself up with "I should haves"

PART 3

Give two examples of things that have happened since you stopped drinking or using that show you that your situation is improving.

PART 4

Explain who or what is your higher power and why you think it can be helpful to you.

STEP 3

"We made a decision to turn our will and lives over to the care of God as we understand Him."

PART 1

Explain how and why you decided to turn your will over to a higher power.

PART 2

Give two examples of things or situations you have turned over in the last week.

PART 3

List two current resentments you have and then explain why it is important for you to turn them over to your higher power.

PART 4

How do you go about "turning over a resentment"?

PART 5

What does it mean to turn your life over to your higher power?

PART 6

Explain how and why you have turned your life over to a power greater than yourself.

STEP 4

"We made a searching and fearless moral inventory of ourselves."

PART 1

List five things you like about yourself.

PART 2

Give five examples of situations where you have been helpful to others.

PART 3

Give three examples of sexual behaviors related to your drinking or using that have occurred in the last 5 years that you feel badly about.

PART 4

Describe how berating yourself for old drinking and using behavior is *not* helpful to your recovery.

PART 5

List five current resentments and explain how holding onto these resentments hurts your recovery.

PART 6

List all laws you have broken related to drinking and using.

PART 7

List three new behaviors you have learned that are helpful to your recovery.

PART 8

List all current fears you are experiencing and then discuss how working the first three steps can help dissolve these fears.

PART 9

Give an example of a situation you have been involved in lately that you handled poorly.

PART 10

Discuss how you plan to handle the situation in Part 9 differently the next time the situation arises.

MODIFIED FOR THE ANTISOCIAL CLIENT

"We admitted we were powerless over alcohol [and drugs]—our lives have become unmanageable."

PART 1

Give five examples of ways you have tried to control your use of chemicals and failed (minimum of 100 words each).

PART 2

Give five examples of people you have tried to control and failed and explain why your controlling behavior was unsuccessful (minimum of 100 words each).

PART 3

Give five examples of situations not associated directly with drinking or using where you have tried to control and failed (minimum of 100 words each).

PART 4

Give two examples of people who have *current* control over you, and explain how that is helpful to you (minimum of 100 words each).

PART 5

Give 10 examples (minimum of 25 words each) of how your drinking and using caused you problems.

PART 6

Give five examples of negative consequences that await you should you continue using drugs or alcohol.

STEP 2

"We came to believe that a power greater than ourselves could restore us to sanity."

PART 1

Repeating the same mistake over and over when you are receiving negative consequences is one definition of insanity. From the list below, identify 15 of your major "mistakes" that lead to wrong thinking. Explain with a minimum of 50 words each how this mistake in your thinking has caused your current problems.

- Excuse making
- Blaming

- Justifying
- Redefining
- Superoptimism
- Lying: commission, omission, assent
- Making fools of others
- Playing the big shot
- Thinking "I'm unique"
- Ingratiating (kissing up)
- Minimizing
- Intentionally being vague
- Using anger and threats
- Playing the victim
- Love for drama and excitement
- Not listening to others
- Maintaining your look good
- Being grandiose
- Intellectualizing

PART 2

List three people you are currently angry at and explain how they can be helpful to you (minimum of 25 words each).

PART 3

List five people more powerful than you who can help you stay clean and sober; explain why (minimum of 50 words each).

PART 4

Who or what is your higher power (minimum of 25 words).

PART 5

Describe how this higher power can help you with your mistakes in thinking (minimum of 100 words).

STEP 3

"We made a decision to turn our will and lives over to God as we understand Him."

PART 1

How did you decide that you needed to turn your will over to a higher power (minimum of 100 words)?

PART 2

Why is it important for you to turn your will over to a higher power (minimum of 50 words)?

PART 3

Explain how you go about "turning it over" (minimum of 50 words).

PART 4

Give three examples of things you have had to "turn over" in the last week (minimum of 50 words).

PART 5

Give three examples of things you have yet to turn over, and explain how and when you plan to do so (minimum of 75 words).

PART 6

What does it mean to "turn your life over to your higher power" (minimum of 100 words)?

PART 7

Without displaying any thinking errors explain how and why you have turned your life over to a power greater than yourself (minimum of 150 words).

STEP 4

"We made a searching and fearless moral inventory of ourselves."

PART 1

List any and all law violations you have committed regardless of whether or not you were caught for these crimes (minimum of 100 words).

PART 2

List every person you have a resentment against and then explain how this resentment is hurting *you* (minimum of 10 examples of 100 words each).

PART 3

Give 10 examples of sexual behavior you engaged in that was harmful to your partner, and explain the negative consequences to *you* for this behavior (minimum of 250 words).

PART 4

Give five examples of aggressive behavior (either verbally or physically) that you have been involved in and explain how it was hurtful to *the other person* and how it was hurtful to *you* (minimum of 250 words).

PART 5

List five major lies you have told and then explain how that lying was hurtful to you (minimum of 250 words).

PART 6

List three lies you have told within the last 48 hours, then explain how this lying hurts your recovery program (minimum of 200 words).

Appendix 2: School Behavior Checklist

Name of student: _____

Teacher: _____ **Class:** _____

Period: _____ **Date:** _____

Please check the following that apply to your observations of the student:

- ☐ Is tardy to class
- ☐ Is absent three or more classes a semester
- ☐ Seems disinterested in school work
- ☐ Appears apathetic and unmotivated to complete assignments
- ☐ Looks tired or sleepy in class
- ☐ Hands in assignments late
- ☐ Doesn't turn in class assignments
- ☐ Is "bored" in class
- ☐ Seems restless in class
- ☐ Appears "spaced out" in class
- ☐ Is disruptive in class
- ☐ Is hanging out with negative peers
- ☐ Has lost interest in school activities
- ☐ Draws drug symbols and signs on papers or clothes
- ☐ Appears angry and guarded
- ☐ Looks sad or depressed
- ☐ Is easily irritated
- ☐ Is more moody than usual

Appendix 3: A Checklist for Parents

HOW TO KNOW IF YOUR CHILD IS USING DRUGS

Your child may be involved with using drugs or alcohol if more than three of the following apply.

Your child is:

- isolating him/herself more than before
- becoming more argumentative with family members
- more secretive about where he/she is going and what he/she is doing
- hanging around with an older group of friends
- seeing different friends than before
- skipping school
- experiencing a drop in grades
- distant and detached from family mdmbers
- feeling restless and "bored" all the time
- no longer interested in previously enjoyed activities
- having contact with the police or juvenile authorities
- in possession of money not easily explained
- taking money and objects from other family members
- displaying a more severe "I don't care" attitude than before
- experiencing a change in sleeping habits
- experiencing a change in eating habits

Appendix 4: Home Behavior Contract*

BEHAVIORAL EXPECTATIONS

1. No verbal abuse or foul language.

2. Homework must be done without hassle.

3. _____ will continue to show good personal hygiene (brushing teeth, hair care, showering, etc.).

4. _____ will keep an appropriately clean room (includes placing dirty laundry in the hamper, making bed in the morning before leaving the house).

5. Table manners will be appropriate.

6. _____ will assist the family with setting and clearing the table.

7. _____ is expected to eat what is served at mealtime without causing a problem.

8. _____will not argue when parents require a haircut.

9. Assigned chores will be completed (per attached schedule).

10. _____ will participate in outpatient therapy with _____ _____ . He/she will report to the session on time.

11. No physical abuse, threats, or intimidation will be tolerated.

---

*Developed by J. Douglas Meyers, Ph.D. and George Howard, M.A.

12. The family will attend family counseling with _____ upon request.

13. _____ will not steal or use other family members possessions without permission.

14. _____ will not be late for chores, from school, to meals, or to any expected activity.

15. The family will participate in a weekly home process meeting on _____ at _____ . The entire family is expected to participate in this meeting unless prior arrangements have been made.

16. Inappropriate teasing and fighting will not be tolerated between brothers and sisters.

17. Family members must state how they feel to other family members.

18. _____ will accept "no" for an answer without causing problems.

DRUG AND ALCOHOL CONTRACT

1. _____ will participate in a minimum of four outpatient drug and alcohol meetings per week. (This can include A.A., N.A., or other structured outpatient D & A group).

2. _____ will find an A.A. or N.A. sponsor within 2 weeks of discharge from the program.

3. _____ will agree to cooperate with providing random urinalysis upon request (by either the parent or outpatient D & A program).

HOME SCHEDULE

	WEEKDAY	WEEKEND
LEVEL I		
LEVEL II		
LEVEL III		

LEVEL SYSTEM

LEVELS OF REINFORCEMENTS

1. **LEVEL I**
   Room restriction for 24 hours. _____ must stay in his/ her room unless at school, doing required chores, or attending an A.A./N.A. meeting. There are no rewards at this level (including telephone, TV, radio, etc.); 24 hours of compliant behavior warrants a level increase to status II at parent's discretion. Written assignments may be requested by family members at this level.

2. **LEVEL II** (48 hours)
   On property privileges:
   TV
   Phone calls
   Visit by friends
   Family outings

   _____

   _____

3. **LEVEL III**
   Full privilege status:
   VCR movies
   Theater movie
   Visit at a friend's house (time limit determined by parents)
   Special family events
   Spending the night at a friend's house

   _____

   _____

   _____

DEMOTION OF A LEVEL STATUS

Any of the following behaviors will result in a drop in status as follows:

A. Verbal abuse	Level I for 24 hours
B. Physical threats or abuse	Level I for 48 hours
C. Lying	Level I for 72 hours
D. School behavior problems	Level decreased to next level for 24 hours
E. Stealing	Level I for 24 hours; written assignments; no TV for 7 days
F. Basic noncompliance with contracted behavioral expectations	Drop to the next level
G. Persistent negative attitude	Drop to the next level
H. Dirty UA	Level I for 7 days; 30 A. A. /N. A. meetings in 30 days
I. Run Away (AWOL)	3 hours of Level I for every hour AWOL
J. Other	To be negotiated

Glossary of Special Terms

This glossary contains definitions for terms that are relatively uncommon or that we have used in unique ways.

Dual diagnosis: A substance abuse/dependency disorder and a coexisting psychiatric disorder requiring simultaneous treatment.

Eskimo: An individual who has a beneficial influence and serves as a vehicle for a "Higher Power" to guide a a person.

Failsafe process: Identifying triggers likely to prompt a relapse and alternate behavior likely to prevent a relapse.

Labeling: Referring to clients or having clients refer to themselves as alcoholics or addicts and/or as persons with a particular psychiatric disorder.

Lapse: Recurrence of a symptoms of a disorder.

Lever: External consequences applied to motivating a client to enter or stay in treatment.

Outside-in strategy: Using treatment strategies that start with environmental interventions, then behavioral, and finally cognitive-expressive ones, depending on the client's current functional level.

Process comments: Statements about the client's defenses or the process in the counseling relationship. This does not deal with specific content of the discussion.

Psychological emancipation: Achieving emotional and cognitive detachment from parents or other relationships.

Recovery model: A theory and treatment approach to substance abuse and dependency that relies on the notions of disease process and the need for abstinence, attendance at Alcoholics Anonymous or similar groups, and the use of step work to achieve sobriety and serenity.

Recovery plan: Proposed client actions likely to promote recovery, including attendance at treatment programs and self-help groups.

Relapse: Responding to lapses with old solutions likely to result in a return to pretreatment status.

Sponsor: A member of Alcoholics Anonymous who serves as a guide and support person in working the Twelve Step program.

Stages of recovery: Process of shifting priorities from an early emphasis on sobriety and stability to a later emphasis on rehabilitation and growth.

Stepwork: Verbal and written exercises designed to internalize the attitudes found in the Twelve Steps of Alcoholics Anonymous.

Survivor: A term used to highlight the positive characteristics of a victim of abusive family experiences.

Thinking errors: A distorted cognitive style that permits individuals to deny responsibility for their behavior.

Index

Alcoholics Anonymous (*continued*)
   required attendance at meetings
      of, 33, 145, 148
   and schizophrenic persons, 75
   sponsorship, 20, 28
   Twelve Steps of, 17–20; *see also*
      Twelve Step recovery model
Alliance for the Mentally Ill, 72, 135
Alzheimer's disease, 87, 91
Anger, 30
   in alcoholism, 14, 46
   in child abuse, 9, 62
   in personality disorder, 96, 98
Antabuse®, 14
Antianxiety medications, 73, 85
Anticholinergic agents, 73
Antidepressant medications, 81
   for panic attacks, 86
Antiharm contracts, 65, 106
Antipsychotic medications, 70, 73,
   92
Antisocial personality disorder, 23,
   30, 96, 100–104
   characteristics of, 98, 101, 146
   and denial, 47
   and gangs, 148
   and head trauma, 89
   modified stepwork for, 170–174
   rates of, 56
   resulting from abuse, 118
   self–world relationship in, 101,
      103
   and substance abuse, 3, 35, 43,
      55, 56
   therapy for, 102–103
   thinking errors in, 102, 103, 104,
      118
Anxiety disorder, 55, 83–87
   generalized, 83, 85
   management skills for, 26, 85
   medication for, 85
   panic attacks in, 86
   prognosis for, 87
   and substance abuse, 3, 85–86
Assertiveness training, 17, 22, 82,
   106

Assuming, 45
Attention-deficit disorder, 89, 91,
   92, 120
   and stimulants, 92, 93
Aversive conditioning, 5, 14

B

BEAM machine, 66
Beattie, Melodie, 131
Behavior contract, 135–136
Benzodiazepines
   addictive nature of, 73
   withdrawal from, 59, 87–88
Biopsychosocial model, 21–22, 24
Bipolar disorder, 23, 75–79
   in adolescents, 122–123
   grief work in, 78, 79
   and lithium carbonate, 24, 60, 61,
      75, 78, 79
   medical compliance in, 75, 78
   modified stepwork for, 165–167
   prognosis for, 79
   and substance abuse, 3, 56
Black, Claudia, 131, 132
Blackouts, 48
Blaming, 44, 117, 118
Borderline personality disorder, 23,
   26, 58, 62, 96
   in adolescents, 121–122
   ambivalence in, 104–105
   characteristics of, 98
   modified stepwork for, 167–170
   prognosis for, 109
   self–world relationship in, 105
   therapy for, 106
Brain damage, 62, 115; *see also*
   Organic mental disorder
Breath analysis, 50
Buspar®, 86

C

Checklist for Parents, 177
Chemical abuse, dependency; *see*
   Substance abuse